ECCENTRICS in CORNWALL

June Lander

'One should always be a little improbable'
Oscar Wilde

Bossiney Books

First published in 1983
by Bossiney Books
St Teath, Bodmin, Cornwall
Designed, typeset and printed in Great Britain by
Penwell Ltd, Parkwood, Callington
Cornwall

ISBN 0 906456 76 2

PLATE ACKNOWLEDGEMENTS

Cover drawing by Paul Honeywill
Pages 5, 7, 19, 50, 53, 56, 86, 92 Ray Bishop
Pages 11, 15, 68, 71, 74, 77, 80 David Woods
Page 22 Earl Davies
Page 25 June Lander
Pages 26, 29 by courtesy of Canon Andrews
Page 33 The Western Morning News
Pages 37, 39 John Rapson
Pages 40, 42, 43 by courtesy of Eric Putnam
Page 47 Paul Broadhurst
Page 59 by courtesy of Sean Dorman
Pages 9, 63, 64, 65, 66, 67 René Halkett
Pages 72, 81 by courtesy of the Bishop of Truro
Page 88 by courtesy of Spencer Thorn
Page 98 George Ellis

About the Author—and the Book

The author started in journalism as a reporter on the *Bath Evening Chronicle,* after being educated in the neighbouring town of Bradford-on-Avon. She subsequently joined the staff of the *Derby Evening Telegraph,* where she met her husband, Hugh, who was also a reporter.

She worked in London as the editor of an international photo-feature agency, syndicating picture stories to newspapers and magazines in Europe and America.

For the last twenty years she has lived in West Cornwall, always in old houses—an interest she shares with her husband, who writes and advises on the subject—and for some years she worked as the County Secretary and Press Officer of the Cornwall W.I. Federation.

She is now a columnist on the staff of *The Western Morning News,* writing on a wide range of topics from comment to conservation and from features to special interviews; touching on her particular interests of art, antiques, authors, Cornish customs and country living.

All this gives plenty of scope for her consuming interest in people—their quirks and passions, talents and bizarre contradictions of character.

So perhaps it is not surprising that for her first book she has chosen to write about eccentrics—those delightful people who add the quality of the unexpected to life.

The author realises that the personalities she has highlighted represent only a small percentage of the colourful characters living in Cornwall—now or in the past—and expects to be told of many she has missed.

Introduction by Colin Wilson

'Eccentricity exists particularly in the English, partly, I think, because of that peculiar and satisfactory knowledge of infallibility that is the hallmark and birthright of the British nation.' So says Edith Sitwell in her delightful book on the English eccentrics. She should have been something of an authority on the subject, for her father, Sir George, was eccentric to the point of dottiness. For those who would like to know more about that gloriously ineffectual and comic character, I recommend the autobiographies of Osbert Sitwell.

In *Eccentrics in Cornwall* June Lander has somehow managed to get some living people to be interviewed on the admission that they're real eccentrics: no easy feat. Interestingly, none of the presentday characters featured are Cornish-born. Does that mean that the Cornish, long-time Non-Conformists, are beginning to conform? Or is the twentieth century making it increasingly difficult to be eccentric? Certainly in the past Cornwall, remote and Celtic, seemed a natural breeding ground for eccentricity. Better communication and 'education' however have changed all that.

We all love the idea of eccentrics because they appeal to the element of the anti-authoritarian in all of us. It is essential, of course, that the eccentric should be in most ways a normal and dignified character—a genuine madman with straws in his hair would not qualify. We laugh at the remarks of the Revd Spooner ('Our Lord *is* a shoving Leopard', 'We all know what it is to have a half warmed fish inside us') because they were genuinely unintentional. And I still recall with wry amusement a delightful and absent-minded old

'Certainly in the past Cornwall, remote and Celtic, seemed a natural breeding ground for eccentricity.'▶

lady who lived in South Kensington, who, when I had been to see her grandson, wandered out of her room completely naked, pinned me in a corner of the stairs, and proceeded to explain to me why she disagreed with my views on Swedenborg. When she had finished, she went back into her room, brought out a copy of Swedenborg's selected writings, which she presented to me (I still have it) then wandered off again, apparently not having noticed that she had nothing on.

My own favourite eccentric is Bernard Shaw's Uncle Barney, described in the Preface to his novel *Immaturity,* whose drinking was so heavy that 'a man who made a bet that he would produce Barney sober, and knocked him up at six in the morning with that object, lost his bet'. Then, quite suddenly, Uncle Barney became a teetotaller, and devoted himself to a monstrous wind instrument called the ophicleide. He also became religious, and used to sit with a Bible on his knees and a pair of binoculars to his eyes, watching the ladies' bathing place at Dalkey. He died in a spectacularly eccentric manner; after going insane and alleging that he was the Holy Ghost, he tried to commit suicide by closing a carpet bag on his head and collapsed from heart failure.

It is also important to remember that eccentricity may be purely in the eye of the beholder. The father of the 'witch' Gerald Gardner, a wealthy landowner, used to remove his clothes every time it rained, and sit on them until the rain stopped. That sounds mad enough. But as anyone who has ever been caught in a shower on the beach will know, the feeling of rain on the naked skin is delightful, and there can be no earthly reason why a man with a taste for it should not sit naked in the rain on his own lawn. Sitting on his clothes sounds odd until we reflect that it would keep them dry, and provide a soft cushion for the naked behind.

Another case in point was an old gentleman called Goodall, whom I met in December 1954, when I was working as a sorter at the post office during the Christmas rush. Mr Goodall had been immortalised by Noel Coward in the song 'Mad Dogs and Englishmen'; when Coward had been in some British outpost in Malaya, he had seen Mr Goodall sitting out in the midday sun without a topee. But the reason was thoroughly prosaic. Mr Goodall had some kind of odd skin rash on the top of his head, and the doctor had recommended him to expose it to strong sunlight. If Coward knew about this he preferred to ignore it; it was much more fun to believe that

'What Cornwall does provide is an atmosphere where eccentricity can flourish.'

'. . . while the English are effete
They're quite impervious to heat.'

And finally, a warning note. Eccentrics *sound* marvellously funny, just as the Marx brothers' visual gags look funny on the screen; in real life, they would only be infuriating. For we must recognise that eccentricity depends on a certain unconscious self-centredness. Sir George Sitwell's eccentricity was rather less amusing when his wife got herself into serious debt with money lenders—largely due to her husband's meanness; he not only declined to pay them but allowed her to go to prison. On the whole, I think it is probably better to read about eccentrics than to live with them.

Who is an Eccentric?

Mention the word 'eccentric' to someone—and I find you always get a positive reaction. It's a sure-fire way of capturing your listener's attention at a party or social gathering. There is a quickening of interest from most people, and it is clear that for the British the word has an obvious appeal.

But you have to be careful how you use it.

From my researches I have come to the conclusion that the divisions—broadly speaking—are as follows:

Those who are eccentric, and are not aware of it.

Those who are eccentric, and are very well aware of it.

Those who would like to be thought eccentric.

Those who would be offended at the suggestion.

I tried it out on my husband, and either because he is too much of an individualist—refusing to be categorised—or he was just being awkward, he didn't agree he was any of them. He did say, however, that if he had a lot of money, he would definitely do a lot more things on whim, which would probably be thought rather bizarre.

Convention has such a strong hold over most of us that any deviation from the norm brings such suggestions as 'he has a screw loose' or 'he is a bit potty', 'round the bend' or 'round the twist'. This coincides with the definition of 'eccentric' given by most dictionaries as meaning 'off centre'.

I found it interesting to compare the definitions from several sources. *The Shorter Oxford Dictionary* of 1977 said of people that it meant 'odd or whimsical'. *Chambers Twentieth Century Dic-*

A drawing by René Halkett: 'I became a perpetual journey-man of life observing and absorbing all this amazing century has to offer.'▶

tionary (1960), which is a great favourite of mine, said it was someone 'not conforming to common rules—odd'. *Websters Third International Dictionary* of 1966 gave eccentric as 'a person who deviates from conventional or accepted conduct, especially in odd or whimsical ways'. They gave as an example: 'An eccentric who cluttered his estate with statues of himself'—presumably all right for Royalty, but not the hoi polloi!

As far as the Cornish are concerned, I'm not sure that eccentricity is a native characteristic—but I'm willing to be proved wrong! Obviously there are eccentrics to be found among the indigenous population, but on the whole I think the Cornish have too much commonsense and pragmatism for it to be accepted as a typically Cornish trait. I am concerned, however, that those fighting for the retention of the true Cornish identity are very often thought to be eccentric—which I find food for thought—especially in an age where standardisation is a creeping, insidious disease.

Setting that aside, what Cornwall does provide is an atmosphere where eccentricity can flourish. It has been a haven for writers and artists for well over a century—both occupations tending to attract a high proportion of eccentrics. Cornwall has always prided itself on its separateness and individuality—aided by the fact that it is practically an island, being almost cut off from England by the length of the River Tamar.

Cornwall is different. You feel it as soon as you step on Cornish soil. Cornishmen wax lyrical, and speak of 'coming home' when they cross the wide expanse of water between Plymouth and Saltash—while one Cornishman assured me recently that when he enters Cornwall via Launceston he notices an immediate change in the quality of the light. Cornwall's very remoteness—gradually diluted by the coming of the railway in the nineteenth century and the motorcar ever since—has meant that the county has kept its identity more than most.

But side by side with the destructive elements which are eating away Cornwall's uniqueness, there is an upsurge in things Cornish: the language is being revived; the Cornish tartan is being worn; the Cornish flag flies on public buildings on St Piran's Day; the Cornish Gorsedd, revived in 1928, continues to meet every September, with the bards in their flowing blue robes providing a colourful and unusual ceremony; and the fight to recognise the power of the Stannary Parliament is continuing.

The Lord Protector of the Stannaries, Brian Hambly, is a bus driver from St Austell. Many people think the determined pursuit of his cause is very eccentric, and over the years has received a great deal of publicity. In his attempt to gain recognition for the Stannary Court, which dates from a charter granted to the tinners in the thirteenth century by Richard, Earl of Cornwall, the matter was brought before the local magistrates by a member who refused to pay his road fund licence; the Queen has been petitioned; the case brought before Lord Justice Widgery in the High Court, and when I spoke to Mr Hambly he was preparing to go to the International Court of Justice.

A link still exists with the Duchy's council, through the Lord Warden of the Stannaries, but so far Prince Charles has avoided taking part in the controversy. As the Duke of Cornwall, however, the Prince still has the power to appoint the High Sheriff in the county, and possesses the gift of a number of church livings.

The Tinner's Saint is St Piran, who must be one of the original

'Cornwall is different. You feel it as soon as you step on Cornish soil.'

eccentrics. He was born in Ireland, where he is supposed to have fed ten kings and their armies for ten days on three cows; raised from the dead soldiers slain on the battlefield and revived hounds killed in the hunt.

Some of the kings decided he was too much of a threat to their authority, so on a stormy day Piran was bound up and chained to a millstone, which was then hurled from the top of a high cliff in the teeth of a tremendous storm. As Piran hurtled down to certain death, the sun suddenly broke through, the wind died down and the water became calm. Instead of plunging to the bottom of the seabed, Piran's millstone became his boat, and he sailed away—landing safely on a beach, which was named Perranporth after him.

There, he built himself a cell and a small church among the dunes and the Cornish flocked to hear his teachings. His first converts were a fox, a badger and a bear. He is said to have lived until he was 206, when he died in a state of drunkenness—still possessing all his teeth and with perfect eyesight.

There have always been rebels in Cornwall not willing to conform. In 901, Edwin the Elder founded the bishopric of Crediton, annexing to it Pawton, Callington and Lawhitton 'that the bishop might thrice a year visit the Cornish to extirpate their errors'—for many apparently still resisted Catholic authority, and clung to the customs of the old British church. This 'clinging to the church' was a recurring feature up to the time of Methodism, which obviously appealed to the Cornish, because they flocked to it in droves.

The unlikely combination of a lawyer and a blacksmith brought about the Cornish Rebellion of 1497 when the Cornish Army marched on London. Three months later, the Cornish swam against the tide when they supported Perkin Warbeck after he landed near Land's End and proclaimed himself Richard IV, and again when they were largely for the King's cause in the Civil War.

Tradition dies hard in Cornwall and Liberalism has held sway here far longer than in most other parts of the country. Until the last election two of the five MPs were Liberal, and the county still has one of the few Liberals in Parliament—David Penhaligon of Truro, who brings a breath of Cornish humour to the proceedings when he addresses the House.

The County Council too can boast that it is the only Independent Council left in the country.

Long Live Eccentrics

If you are looking for eccentrics, where do you find them? I talked with Mr Leslie Douch, curator of the County Museum in Truro. He said the museum attracts eccentrics, but he believes that genuine eccentrics 'flower unseen, or have a little circle where they are tolerated or appreciated', but as many who come to the museum are his friends, he did not think it was possible to mention any by name.

Obsessionists, he said, were easier to spot. He remembered one man who had elaborate maps, and was trying to prove that all iron-age forts could be pinpointed by drawing circles of a certain diameter over the whole of Cornwall.

'He missed out a lot of iron age camps in the process, and I couldn't persuade him that he was wrong.'

We discussed the difference between being 'an eccentric' and being 'a character'. He thought there was a fine distinction.

He was sure too that in their time inventors like Goldsworthy Gurney and Humphry Davy must have appeared eccentric.

'Was he eccentric,' I asked?

'I hope so,' he said. 'I've always been told that I am the one who is supposed to do daft things, and it is in doing daft things that one gets the fun out of life—as long as you don't offend or affect other people.'

As the son of an undertaker in Wimborne, he used to see the professional mourners, who loved to go to funerals. They got intense enjoyment out of judging the style of each one, counting the number who came, and who they were. He remembered two old spinsters—Pop and Dodger—whose main occupation in life was to go to such ceremonies. 'Got any jobs in?' they would ask his father. As a boy he vividly recollects playing at boats in the open coffins!

His final verdict was that if a person is deliberately playing to an audience then they aren't really eccentric. This conclusion is perhaps a little harsh—but we will see.

This brings me to my own definition, which is that an eccentric is someone who does what he wants to do, despite convention. I personally believe that eccentrics are born, not made, and that even if pronounced eccentricity does not appear until later in life, the seeds are there from an early age.

'Doing what he wants to do, despite convention' can therefore take many forms, according to people's tastes and inclinations, which is why we have so many different types of eccentrics.

For instance, why are there so many eccentric clergymen, especially in the Church of England? Piers Brendon, who wrote *Hawker of Morwenstowe,* the biography of a noted eccentric parson, points out that 'the established church in the nineteenth century, especially in rural areas, gave men, thus inclined, unique opportunities to cultivate their eccentricities.' I have therefore devoted a whole chapter to eccentric parsons of the past, as well as two eccentric parsons who were friends.

I asked the present Bishop of Truro, the Rt. Rev. Peter Mumford, how many eccentric clergymen he knew. Without hesitation he said: 'Lots and lots of them'.

To Bishops their eccentric clergy can be 'a great trial', he said.

The Bishop of Truro in 1912 could obviously see what was coming when he inducted the Rev. Bernard Walke to St Hilary Church in West Cornwall because, as Walke wrote in his book *Twenty Years at St Hilary,* he preached 'a thinly veiled warning' against his extreme practices.

The Bishop had previously done his best to deflect him, because when Walke asked him for a living he had replied that 'good men are needed in the North'!

I read Bishop Mumford the start of my chapter on 'Parson Eccentrics' and asked him if what I had said was true—that parsons could still do more or less what they liked.

He agreed it was. 'They have tremendous freedom,' he said. Then, with a twinkle, he told me: 'They can be lazy, drunken or adulterous—but they would have to be awfully indolent, awfully drunk or awfully adulterous before being thrown out.'

The Author visiting St Hilary's Church.▶

As far as services are concerned, he said, the clergyman gives a solemn oath to take the services by law provided. Up until fairly recently he could almost take what services he liked within the law, and to this day he still has a lot of licence. He is bound to recite morning and evening prayers every day. 'It doesn't say it has to be in church, but the hope is that it will be, so that people can come and join him.' He is also bound on Sundays to conduct services in his parish, made more difficult nowadays because a lot of priests have more than one church to administer.

He said it is all summed up in Dale's Law (of the Parish Church), but since 1965 certain alternative services have been permitted—although the obligation for morning and evening prayer and Holy Communion remains the same. He also has to consult his Church Council about any changes, variations or experiments with the services.

The Bishop thought there were several reasons why there were more eccentrics in the Church of England than in other churches, but one of the most important was the matter of the parson's freehold. This guaranteed him independence—once instituted, hardly anything could move him. It went back to the Parochial System, he said, when the priest was protected—first of all from the Barons, then from the Bishops and finally in the nineteenth century from the squires. A lot of landowners still hold the patronage of livings—especially in Cornwall. Other patrons include the Bishops, the Queen, the Prince of Wales—Stoke Climsland and Lanteglos by Camelford, for instance, are in his gift—and the Oxford Colleges.

'The freehold meant the priest was protected from being sacked or pushed around—and their subsequent attitude of "you can't get rid of me" was all part of the English tradition of fierce independence,' he said.

'The parson's freehold is very jealously guarded. The Bishops want to get rid of it, so they can sack the duds, and it is a perennial point of discussion. At the moment the whole thing is fraught with tremendous checks and balances which have grown up over the years.'

The Methodist Church, he said, has the rule of Conference, whereby, every September at their Annual Conference, there is the 'great turn round', when it is decided which Ministers should move and where. The Roman Catholic Church has no system of patronage. There the Bishops decide themselves about the movement of their men. 'The C of E is of course very much the product of the English nation, and the English genius for compromise and freedom.'

Asked for his own examples of eccentric clergy, he mentioned the man in Norfolk, whose wife suddenly rang up the Archdeacon one day, and said: 'It's desperate—you had better come, he's after me with a carving knife.'

'The Archdeacon arrived at the isolated rectory, parked his car at the bottom of the drive, and crept up through the bushes, until he heard a great caterwauling inside. He peered cautiously through the dining room window, and there was the priest chasing his wife round the table with a carving knife. The Archdeacon watched fascinated for a few moments, and then suddenly the Rector spotted him, and said: "What are you doing here, Archdeacon, bastard? Go away." The Archdeacon managed to leap through the window, overpower the chap, and lead him away in an hysterical condition.'

A parson's study, he said, told you a lot about him. He remembered one man in Bedfordshire, who lived in a rather fine house, asking him to come into his study. 'He opened the door, and you were at once ankle deep in sawdust. The whole room was full of works of carpentry—lathes, electric saws, and all kinds of gadgetry—which of course was not doing the floor and walls any good.'

There was the man who made a tremendous fuss about his personal health, and would jump up and down from the table several times during a dinner party, putting on and taking off his waistcoat, according to how his temperature rose and fell during the meal. And the man who used to shave himself with two razors at once—to save time.

'Then there was my own second cousin, two or three times removed—S.Baring Gould, the great hymn writer, who had a very large number of children, fourteen I think it was. He was a wealthy squire's son in Lewtrenchard in Devonshire—and the famous story goes of how he loved children—you'd have to if you had all that number!—and giving them parties, and built a great ballroom onto his house specially. One day he ran into a little child on the staircase, during one of these parties, and said: "And whose little girl are you?" The small child looked up at him, wept, and said: "Yours Papa." '

The Bishop, I'm sure, would like the story of Parson Froude, Vicar of Knowstone in Devonshire, who, hearing that Bishop

Phillpotts of Exeter was coming to look into his ecclesiastical irregularities, had a trench-type booby trap dug in the track up to his vicarage. His ruse succeeded, and the Bishop took a tumble.

Writing in *A Cornishman Abroad* A.L. Rowse gives his own examples of eccentric clergymen. He stayed with Bishop Headlam at the Palace in the Close of Gloucester Cathedral. Calling him 'an episcopal gorilla', he says he was a great disciplinarian and terrorised his clergymen. 'I dare say he had reason to be,' writes Dr Rowse. 'Up in the Cotswold hill parishes parsons mouldered away with too little to do.'

He goes on to tell of one place where the clergyman was at loggerheads with the parishioners, who refused to come to church. 'Headlam was at pains to bring them back again. The parson, having got them safely inside, went down the aisle, locked them all in, and grinned in through the windows at them.'

Another time the Bishop visited one of his retired clergymen. When he was leaving, the man said: 'You see that man over there? He think's he is God!' He then added: 'But how can that be when I am He!'

Comments Dr Rowse: 'O dear old C. of E. where alone such entertaining eccentricities were possible.'

When I went to see A.L. himself just before his 79th birthday, he had forgotten our appointment, and was still in bed, half-way through the morning. Full of apologies, he invited me up to his bedroom, where I talked to him, as he sat with his back against the mahogany headboard, dressed in his pyjamas and a woollen pullover.

I discussed eccentrics with him. 'The literal meaning of the word is "out of centre",' he said, quoting from his old copy of *Nuttalls Standard Dictionary,* bound in brown paper.

'Someone who is irregular or anomalous' he read out.

When we had finished talking he showed me round the house in his dressing-gown and slippers, and we finished up on the lawn, where he pulled out bits of grass by the roots from the gravel approach and carefully pushed them into the edges.

'You will think me eccentric,' he said, 'but I'm not. I'm very

Hawker, a noted eccentric parson, had a hut on these cliffs at Morwenstow where he retreated to write. ▶

practical,' adding that one of the advantages of being working class was that he had 'a lot of commonsense, and was rather down to earth'.

Obviously the odd eccentric act does not make a person eccentric—it has to be part of their persona. My own mother-in-law, for instance, was eccentric. Not that anyone in the family ever actually said she was—when you are close to people and know them intimately over a period of time, you come to accept their characteristics, and no longer question them.

'She was only marginally eccentric in actual behaviour—but deeply eccentric in the core of her personality,' is how my husband put it. 'Anyone observing her for five minutes would soon see she was eccentric—they would see it as a quality of mind,' he added.

Her conversation was certainly rivetting—and the fact that she had a wicked desire to shock—especially prudes or stuffed shirts—meant she would say outrageous things, which produced the desired effect on mild, rather straight-laced people. I remember after she had regaled the company one Sunday evening with her version of the sexual practices of some obscure native tribe, a clergyman friend of mine commiserated with us later in the genuine belief that she was slightly unhinged.

She was a great talker, and had opinions on everything under the sun. Life in the charming old house in which she lived had a Russian tempo. Time had no meaning. Meals were at odd hours, as discussions continued over a late breakfast, more usually telescoped into a combined lunch, because one had been talking into the small hours.

Sent on an errand to Eila—short for Eileen—in her bedroom, it was difficult to get away. In my position as new daughter-in-law, and not being used to such a family, I didn't know how to deal with the situation. Later I learnt how to make a brisk, tactical withdrawal—but was never sure how long the soliloquy went on when I was not there!

Going to bed took ages. Hot water bottles cooled under arms as the talk went on in the large old-fashioned kitchen; to and fro-ing continued between the bedrooms as someone thought of a new point in an argument, or a family matter was pounded out in endless and often quite irrelevant detail.

It was sometimes difficult to keep up with the switches which had taken place during the night. One might go to bed with one thing decided, even if it was only where we were going the next day, to find at breakfast that something completely different had been agreed overnight, and the discussions would start again. They were all pretty strong-minded women in the family, so the effect could be overwhelming.

Summing up his mother my husband said: 'She could be very wilful and unreasonable, and then switch magically into displaying a high degree of sensitivity and wisdom. From being furiously angry and determined about something, she would then have a tremendous change of heart, and being naturally generous would admit she was wrong in the matter.'

As an example of her unconventional behaviour, I remember how, when she became partially disabled, she demonstrated to an astonished friend the use of a 'helping hand'—a metal stick with a claw at the end, which could be operated to pick up things like a newspaper. After showing what she could do with it, she then demonstrated with great determination what she could not do, by sweeping all the saucepans off a top shelf, so that they tumbled to the floor with a tremendous clatter.

She talked to everyone—entering into political discussions with shop assistants as she bought her glasses in Woolworths—an unheard of thing for a person from her social background at that time. As a Land Girl in the First World War she shared a bunk house with girls from the poorest parts of Liverpool, and also rode a motorcycle—a pretty rare sight in 1916. I remember surprising her in the kitchen of a holiday house in Perranuthnoe we took one summer, drinking milk out of the milk jug!

Eila certainly did what she wanted to do, without regard to convention, but because she was by upbringing the conventional product of an Edwardian age she was split down the middle, and suffered accordingly. Her saving graces were her great charm and genuine interest in other people.

Being in journalism is a marvellous way of meeting eccentric people—the zanier the better as far as I am concerned. People doing odd things were the staff of life to us at an International Photo-Feature Agency I worked for in London. Of all the interesting characters I interviewed—the man with the longest handlebar moustache; Earl Lloyd George, son of the famous Prime Minister, living in a pigman's cottage; the showman Duke of Bedford; Peter Blake, the artist, who was then making paintings by riding his bike over canvasses—the man who stands out as the most eccentric is

The Author: 'I am an inveterate collector of the strange and bizarre.'

Gerard Hoffnung. He was another man I interviewed in his dres-singgown and slippers. Well-known as a cartoonist, it was his Interplanetary Music Concert at the Festival Hall, which won him fame at that time.

He told me he had been eccentric in his youth. As a student he would have a meal backwards in a restaurant; ask Members of Parliament for cigarette cards or greet a woman outside a theatre as his long-lost nannie. But now he regarded himself as normal.

His 'normality' took the form of producing an annual musical event in which the instruments included a fat boy blowing on a watering can; his wife on a ship's fog horn; a young girl playing a road rammer; the noise from an Espresso coffee machine; eight Valkyries on scooters, cow bells, pop guns, two ping-pong players who changed places after each volley—and, for persistent coughers in the audience—a machine gun in the wings.

He assured me that the resulting concert was 'for serious musicians by serious musicians', and that they would only employ a vacuum cleaner, a pneumatic drill or a ping-pong table if they had a point musically, not just for the sake of using them!

I am an inveterate collector of the strange and bizarre, and recently this has included a woman in Florida who revealed in a divorce-court hearing that she often went to bed with a three foot trumpet wrapped in a blanket beside her.

'I was probing psychic phenomena, and there is a school of thought which says that the dead will speak to the living through a trumpet,' she explained.

In Penzance a woman in 1982 was planning to produce an eighteenth century play which she had discovered in the Morrab Library. Called '*Chrononhotonthologus*' it is about the King of Queerumania. Another character is the King of the Antipodes—who walks around upside down. 'The part isn't half as difficult as it sounds,' said Mrs Caroline White, an assistant cataloguer at the library. 'We hope the costume will also be made upside down.'

From my own newspaper *The Western Morning News*, Sarah Foot's story about Merryn Longfoot of TSW mentioned that one of Merryn's ambitions was to be 'as eccentric and outspoken' as her Cornish grandmother. Apparently she used to get up and interrupt sermons in the church at Lostwithiel when she wanted to make a point—and always carried a flask of ready-mixed gin and tonic.

I liked the story of the motorist in Chipping Norton who when booked for parking half on and half off double yellow lines in the high street, cut his car in half, and put the front half on the spot where he had been given the ticket. Police removed the decapitated car—only to find that he had dumped the back half on the same spot. A police spokesman said: 'We are now hoping he is quite satisfied, and that this will really be the end of it.'

John Stuart Mill writing *On Liberty* in 1859 said that eccentricity was a valuable counter to the deadening weight of man's conformity in an increasingly democratic society.

'Eccentricity has always abounded, and the amount of eccentricity in a society has generally been in proportion to the amount of genius, mental vigour and moral courage it contained.'

The same is true nearly 130 years later.

All I can say is 'Long Live Eccentrics'.

Canon Andrews

Being eccentric might be said to involve an element of selfishness—doing what *you* want to do, despite convention and the opinion of others.

This is certainly not true of Canon Martin Andrews CVO, MBE, MC. He has spent his very long life tirelessly working for others, and displaying kindness and Christian charity at every step. Even so, eccentric things seem to have happened to him, and his life has been full of the most remarkable incidents.

As a young clergyman he drove one of the first Triumph motorcycles ever to be used on the Queensland border of the Australian bush; rode a donkey called Alphonse in Khartoum while carrying out his religious duties; captained an English Army football team; played tennis at Wimbledon; created jobs for over forty people in Cornwall in the 1930s when there were millions of unemployed and became a close friend of the Royal Family.

I met him at his house in Downderry, not far from the sea, where he now lives in retirement after being Rector of Stoke Climsland from 1922-1970.

'Did you see all those old people on the television the other night?' were his first words to me. Born in 1886, he was, at the time I met him, 96 years old!

He is a relation of Jeannie Tangye, and drawings by her of Minack cottage near St Buryan, where she and Derek live with their animals, were displayed behind him on the wall.

The inside of the house, built about the beginning of the century, and set at the end of a little private road, has a gracious air—achieved by boldly swagged curtains, yellow draped tables, mirrors decorated with shimmering glass pendants and a variety of interesting prints and pictures. In the sitting room, where the Canon gave me coffee, there was attractive cane furniture, pretty

Canon Andrews at his home at Downderry.

cushions and an elaborate fireplace with an overmantel, which he told me had been made up from parts of a Victorian bedstead.

In a niche in the wall behind me was a display of white china, together with a clever arrangement of pale pink artificial magnolias made of silk. This was the work of Vincent Curtis, his companion and right-hand man, who died in 1981. The son of a lorry driver in Stoke Climsland, he joined the Canon soon after leaving school, and was a leading light in the household. He cooked superbly, had a considerable flair for arranging flowers and was a great favourite of the Royal Family. Among the hundreds of letters Canon Andrews received after Vincent died was one from the Queen Mother expressing her personal sympathy.

The Canon showed me a photograph of Vincent, and I admired his dark, good looks. 'I think he was a descendant of a Spanish Duke washed ashore from the Armada,' said the Canon. 'He was very musical and artistic. I once went to Venice with him, and attended a

The Canon with Vincent—'a great favourite of the Royal Family'.

lecture about painting. Vincent spoke up, and said: Hasn't the figure in the right hand corner been added by a later hand? I thought it was a cheek to interrupt, but the man left the platform, put his arms round him and said, "That's what I have been saying all my life, and no-one will believe me," and the rest of the lecture was almost a dialogue between them.'

The Canon was very alert when I met him, working on his second book *Honey And Other Sweet Things,* which takes its title from his beloved Labrador dog.

I digress momentarily with a story about the Canon's father, which to me illustrates the same mixture of kindness and eccentricity. All his children had gone for their annual visit to the pantomime at Drury Lane Theatre, when they noticed a family near them in great distress. Apparently, when the father had changed into his dress clothes, he had left all his money behind. The Canon's father immediately went to the Box Office and paid for the seats of the family of six, who were complete strangers to him. The money was paid back at once, the Canon told me, and every Christmas they received 'the biggest box of chocolates we'd ever seen'.

Martin Andrews will go down in history as the man who really did something about the problem of unemployment in the 1930s. The story begins with a gift of chrysanthemum cuttings from a parishioner in Stoke Climsland. The Canon tried his hand at growing these, never having done so before.

He was so successful, that he was advised to put the subsequent blooms into the local Chrysanthemum Show, where he won third prize. Determined to beat his neighbour, the dentist, who had swept the board, he bought some more cuttings, filled a greenhouse and his large rectory with the plants, and next time was the chief prize-winner at the show. He had grown so many that they filled every available space, and could be seen on ledges in every window.

Not long afterwards a man came to the door, wanting to know if he would sell the flowers to him. The Canon's first reaction was to say no, for they were precious to him after all the care he had lavished on them; but the man said he had been out of work for over a year, and he knew a dealer in Plymouth who would take them.

The Canon's heart was touched, and he sold them—and it was from this point that he determined he would help the unemployed in the parish by growing fruit and flowers, which would give them work. He sold the few shares he possessed, rented sixteen acres of land from the Land Steward of the Duchy of Cornwall, and went to see Fred Rogers, the leading flower expert in the district. He was out, but Mrs Rogers was there, and in a few hours she gave him 'more advice and encouragement than I ever had before or since'. Help on the accounting side came from Herbert Rendell, who had worked in a bank in Launceston.

Soon the Canon was taking on men: some to grow flowers and raise chickens, and others—like carpenters and masons—to make pig and poultry houses, and greenhouses for the tomatoes and flowers. Even when Herbert Rendell shook his head over the size of the overdraft at the bank, Canon Andrews never turned anyone away who wanted a job. As he pointed out, the object was to give men work, not to make a profit.

In the beginning, though, he had the problem of marketing the produce, and it must have been a strange sight to see a parson trying to sell fruit and flowers commercially to the shops.

'It was the most humiliating job of all, and the men who received their wages every week, little knew what I suffered.'

An even better sight must have been the Canon—for he had just been made one—braving the ladies' dress department of the old Dingles store in Bedford Street, Plymouth with a box of flowers to sell in his hand. His objective was the flower stand at the bottom of some stairs in the department. Salvation was, however, at hand—as so often in the Canon's life! The person in front being served was Nancy Dingle. She introduced him to the buyer, Miss Lock, who became one of their best customers.

After four years he was employing over twelve men, but the unemployment figures had unfortunately reached over two million. At this point, a prince arrived in an aeroplane. It was the Prince of Wales in his red Fox-Moth. He admired the work which had already been done, and said he was interested in expanding the scheme. Unfortunately he was not able to carry out his ambitious plans, but it gave the Canon an opportunity to rent some more Duchy property, and to grow strawberries and daffodils for the Covent Garden firm of George Munro.

The Prince continued to visit the farms and give encouragement, and it was on one of these visits that he picked out a puppy from a litter of Old English Sheepdogs on the estate, who was promptly named Punch—his mother being called Judy. Punch became an outstanding character, and was responsible for a 'great ecclesiastical episode'.

One Sunday, when the church door had been left wide open, because it was a warm, sunny evening, and the sidesmen were processing up the aisle with the collection, Punch was seen following behind with a large bone in his mouth. After the presentation of the alms plate, Punch came forward and dropped the succulent bone at his master's feet. He waited while the alms were offered, then turned round with the sidesmen and proceeded down the aisle of the church. This incident gave the Canon a wonderful text for his sermon the following Sunday, on 'giving more than thy all'.

Because of his links with the Duchy Estates, Canon Andrews got to know many members of the Royal Family, and was asked to preach in the chapel at Buckingham Palace before King George V and Queen Mary. As so often in the Canon's life, it turned out to be a momentous occasion. It was January, 1924. Baldwin's Conservative Government had been defeated in the Commons, and the King had sent for Ramsay MacDonald to be the first Socialist Prime Minister in the history of Parliament. The situation had set the Establishment by the ears—members of the Peerage hurried up to London, while the Archbishop of Canterbury was already there.

'I was staying with the King's Private Secretary, Lord Stamfordham, and I heard his daughter telling all the illustrious callers that her father had an engagement, and couldn't see anyone.' Obviously the Canon's visit was a good cover, so that Lord Stamfordham could avoid any potentially embarrassing meetings.

The Canon had been instructed to keep his sermon short—in fact to fourteen minutes precisely. 'If you preach less, the king may say you were too lazy to prepare it, if you preach more, he will say you don't know when to stop.' He was also advised to read his sermon.

When the moment came, he climbed the steps of the pulpit as if

The Queen and Prince Philip visit Cornwall.
Canon Andrews is on the left.

going to be beheaded, dropped his prepared sermon after the first page, and had to extemporise. In his agitation he realised he was shouting, so brought it hurriedly to a close. It must have gone better than he thought, because the King told his Secretary: 'Thank God you have at last sent me a man I can hear, and who knows when to stop.'

The Canon entertained the Prince at the Rectory, went to receptions in London at which he was present, and visited him at Fort Belvedere. He was also invited to have drinks with him at the flat of Mr & Mrs Simpson in Bryanston Court. There the Prince talked to him alone, quoting, to his astonishment, detailed figures of the number of people out of work in the towns and villages of Cornwall.

'He was the most popular man ever, and was genuinely keen on finding work for the unemployed,' reminisced the Canon.

When the Royal Party, including the Simpsons, had a holiday at the Carlyon Bay Hotel, and then came to lunch with the Canon, all eyes were on Wallis Simpson. 'She was a quiet person, who dressed with great taste. But she could become gay and vivacious, and talk with ease on every subject—sometimes most amusingly,' said the Canon.

After that day the Canon was convinced that the Prince was deeply in love with Mrs Simpson. The implications of this situation were so great that he decided to impart his fears to the then Prime Minister, Stanley Baldwin. He was the first to tell him, and got the impression that he found it hard to believe. Later when the Prince became King he came to Stoke Climsland and had a long talk with the Canon, who was his chaplain—the only one he appointed. The Abdication came as a great sorrow to him, especially as it meant he would be unable to visit them and take a close interest in their schemes.

Other Royal visits came in later years. King George VI and Queen Elizabeth; the Queen and Prince Philip; Princess Margaret; the Duke and Duchess of Kent and the Duke and Duchess of Gloucester.

The visit of King George VI is especially remembered by the Canon because of The Case of The Disappearing Soap, and the vegetable served at lunch. Preparing for Royal visits, especially if the personages concerned are to dine with you, can be quite an ordeal. Luckily the Canon had all the right friends. He borrowed the butler from Werrington Park; two waiters from the Carlyon Bay

Hotel, who were rumoured to have served President Roosevelt and Winston Churchill in North Africa, and asked a friend at the Electricity Board for help. The Board put heaters in all the rooms, fitted an extra cooker, made sure the system wasn't overloaded and sent an electrician for the day to keep an eye on things.

The King had to change into his Naval uniform for his afternoon engagement in Plymouth, so the Canon gave him his room—with a rug over the hole in the carpet—and put special soap in the bathroom opposite. Later when checking that all was in order, he found that his rose-scented soap had been cast aside, and a small piece of cheap soap substituted. He hurled this into a spare room, and replaced it with his original fragrant tablet.

Just as the party were lined up to receive the Royal guests, the King's valet told him he was in great trouble. Someone had taken the King's soap—the soap the King particularly liked, and took everywhere with him on his travels. The Canon rushed upstairs, retrieved the soap from the dark corner into which he had thrown it, and put it next to his own piece. Later he was relieved to hear that the visit had been thought a great success, including the soap!

Earlier though there had nearly been a disaster over the vegetables. Despite growing their own, the beans were found to be stringy.

'Why not use the Savoys?' suggested the Canon.

'Give the King cabbage?' was the astonished reply of Vincent Curtis.

'Why not?' said the Canon. 'You must have heard of cabbages and kings.'

The Queen was delighted when she saw what had been prepared. 'The King will be pleased,' she said. 'He loves cabbage, and we so seldom have it, except at home.'

When he first arrived at Stoke Climsland Rectory in 1922, friends had commented that they would give him six weeks 'in that outlandish place in the wilds of Cornwall'.

The house was unfurnished. All he possessed was a roll-top desk, his own personal luggage and six tennis rackets. Not much to fill 27 rooms! So he set off for a sale being held at Trenython, the home of the late Bishop Gott. Because everything seemed to be going for high prices, he found it difficult to start bidding. Then up came a grand piano. He started to bid, thinking it would fill space, and the young people from the village could play it. He got it for £16.

Next a bagatelle board caught his eye. That would do if he started a club for the young, he thought. In the same lot he had purchased several footmen's uniforms, in very good condition, a dilapidated wine cooler and a contraption for making cider. He realised that those at the sale must be wondering what sort of establishment he was going to set up! Especially when he found at the end he hadn't bought any beds, tables or chairs, but masses of oil lamps, useless coffee pots, old stoves, which could never work, and quantities of fenders, pokers, tongs and butler's trays.

The Canon had started his ministry after he was ordained by accepting a posting to the Brotherhood of the Good Shepherd at Dubbo in New South Wales. On the voyage to Australia in a ship of the White Star line, which was scheduled to take six weeks, there was one of those strange happenings which seem to have dogged his life.

During the trip he found himself Crossing The Line on Christmas Day. Soon after this the Captain told him that a man had died, and he would like him to bury him at sea just before midnight. Then before tea a Presbyterian minister had a fight with a fellow passenger, because he had sworn at him. At the end of the day, as he was gazing up at the stars after the impressive funeral, a man came up to him and shook his hand. 'May I congratulate you? Few can say—on Christmas Day I crossed the line, saw a parson have a fight and buried a man on the Equator!'

He discovered that Brewarrina, where he was bound, was regarded as a great joke in the area. 'It's so hot there' he was told, 'that you have to feed the chickens ice-cream to stop them laying hard-boiled eggs!'

To travel across this parish, which was thousands of miles square, he left for the bush the morning after he arrived on a four-week trip in a buggy with two half-broken horses. Later he was to drive a new Triumph motorcycle—one of the first ever to be used in the bush.

He was initially due to visit townships on the Queensland border, mining camps and sheep stations, where a parson hadn't been seen in months. At one station, for something to say to the waiting family, he looked at the overcast sky and remarked: 'I am afraid we are going to have some rain.' 'I never lived it down,' he told me. The area was in the middle of a drought, and they had been praying for rain for ten months!

Weddings could be rather rowdy affairs, especially in a mining

The Canon's horticultural schemes provided jobs for the unemployed in the 1930s.

area, developing into a free fight afterwards with both sides finishing up in gaol. The custom of being the first to kiss the bride often meant the roughest customer got there first. A bush parson friend, determined not to let this happen at one wedding, noticed a burly bushman creeping up on the bride. When he got to the words 'let no man put asunder' he landed an uppercut with his left on the man's jaw, which laid him out, much to everyone's delight.

When the First World War broke out, the Canon couldn't get a passage back to England, so he joined up as a stretcher bearer with the Australian Army. They travelled from Sydney in a Chinese transport ship, and approaching the equator, he was told by the medical officer that he was going to have to operate on a man with appendicitis at midnight, when the captain would stop the ship, and would he give the anaesthetic? He protested that he didn't know what to do—but the doctor said he would instruct him as they went along.

So at midnight, with four perspiring Australians fanning them with towels, he gave the man chloroform under the doctor's orders.

The operation was successful, but when by chance he met the young doctor again later in France, he confessed that it had been his first operation, and the man hadn't even had appendicitis!

In Egypt he was part of the advance party which had to march to Cairo. The sergeant major made it clear that no-one should fall out on the march, as it would let the whole unit down. Just as they started, he told me that he began to get violent pains in his stomach, and had to be held up by two men, with his equipment carried by others. In Cairo they took him to a bar and gave him a brandy. He felt a little better so tried some Creme de Menthe, which seemed to relieve the pain. All night long his Australian friends dosed him with Creme de Menthe and brandy. In the train to Alexandria next morning he slept like a log, and woke up feeling very fit. He was able to march on to the transport ship, while his pals collapsed on the deck, worn out by their all-night ministrations.

'I reckon you ought to patent your cure for Gippy Tummy,' said one, 'you would make your fortune.'

His captaining of an English football side came after the Armistice of the First World War. 'We had a number of professional footballers in our side—well-known men who had been called up. We played the Belgians—I was centre half—and beat them 3-0. I wanted to leave it at that but the C.O. insisted on a return match. The professionals had been demobbed by then, and I'm afraid we lost 7-0 that time!'

His debut at Wimbledon came in 1921, and although he didn't survive the first rounds on the outside courts, it was whilst playing there that he received a letter saying that the living of Stoke Climsland, which was in the gift of the Prince of Wales, was vacant, and would he accept it if offered? He couldn't at the time, because of his work in Sudan, but after another six months there, a war wound started to give him trouble. He returned to England on doctor's advice, and after much thought, agreed to go to the living in Cornwall.

Years later he entertained Australian Air Force men on leave during the Second World War at the Rectory. He found them restive and on edge—until he hit on the idea of playing poker with them, which they found very relaxing.

Later still one Easter Monday he received a visit from the man who had asked if he could buy his first chrysanthemums all those years before, which had given him the idea of starting the scheme for the unemployed. He had done well, his son was at public school, and he had promised his wife that one day he would bring her to Stoke Climsland to see the flowers at Easter. Before leaving, he gave the Canon a cheque as a donation to the fabric fund of the church.

The Canon's whole life is summed up in this story. He was eccentric enough to follow his own instincts and start something unusual. But by casting his bread upon the water, he received it back a thousand-fold.

'Things are never as bad as they seem,' he told me, and this has been his motto all his life.

On my last visit to him, he told me of a wish he would like to see fulfilled. He would like one day set aside as a national Animal Day, with the forget-me-not flower used as the emblem for flags to be sold for charity.

'The flower is the symbol of friendship—and the cause is one which no-one would disagree with in this country, whatever their colour, religion or financial standing. There is a wonderful feeling of sympathy amongst ordinary people for animals' he said.

He has put this idea to several animal charities, and is waiting to hear if it will be taken up.

I do hope it is—it would be a marvellous achievement for a remarkable man, whose life has never been dull, and who, approaching his centenary, is still rooting for others at a time when he might be forgiven for thinking of himself for a change.

Eric Putnam

People may not always agree about what makes an eccentric—but there's not much doubt about Eric Putnam.

Those who come into contact with him instantly recognise that they have met someone out of the ordinary. It may be his habit of always carrying champagne in the boot of his car; of running his Cornish newspaper on modern technological lines, while still retaining old-fashioned advertisements on the front page; or even of answering the telephone at night, when everyone else has gone home, in a Cornish accent pretending to be the caretaker.

His amazing mixture of the very sophisticated and the rather naive leaves most people guessing. Even his style of writing can be a conundrum. It is very individual—but if you are a 'Putters' expert, you can recognise it at once. Cornwall is always 'the Best Country'; Devon is 'the Backward County', whilst those in London are referred to as 'the Redcoats'.

The readers of his newspaper *The Cornish Times* are referred to as 'the Great Family of South East Cornwall', and he never tires of telling how he came to buy the newspaper in the early 1960s. He says his idea was to get rid of it after a year to Harmsworth at a substantial profit—but he fell in love with the paper and the people.

He admits he lost money on it at first, but he made it a viable proposition by throwing out the linotype machines in 1971 and installing computerised setting before any other paper in Cornwall. He gave up editing the paper in 1978, and would be the first to admit that its circulation has increased steadily ever since.

Ask him about the out-of-date practice of putting advertise-

Eric Putnam: Those who meet him recognise they have met someone out of the ordinary. ▶

ALFA ROMEO
OCV
360R

ments—always the same property agents—on the front page, and he will tell you that his readers like it.

'They want to see who is moving, and what properties are on the market.' Then he adds stoutly: 'It's very fine news.'

Later he says revealingly: 'If I changed the front page, it would give people an opportunity to ask themselves—why do I take it?'

This shows the cautious businessman in Eric, working alongside the journalist, who likes to write outrageous things about people, and is genuinely hurt when they take offence. It's not unknown for his office manager to be asked to send bouquets of flowers to women who feel affronted by something he has written, or for other people to be asked out to lunch to make amends. The late author, Mary French, who lived near Liskeard, and who tried to buy the paper from Eric early on, told me that he once sent her an enormous bottle of French scent. She didn't know what to do with it, so hid it behind a bookshelf, and eventually gave it to a bazaar.

On the inside pages the paper does not run to many eye-catching headlines, though a few more 'cross two' and 'cross threes' have been insidiously creeping in under the editorship of John Collings. Eric's philosophy goes like this—the more banner headlines, the less space for news, and I must admit he has a point when I see my Daily Mail front page half-filled with one headline. As a racing man he will tell you: 'If I put 23 stories on a page, the odds are that someone will find something which interests them. Cut down that number—and you cut the odds.' It's a policy which seems to have paid off. As a BBC interviewer commented in a programme on the state of local newspapers in the West in 1982: 'The paper prospers for all the wrong reasons.'

Since giving up the editorship he has written a regular column under the title of 'My Type'—a heading as enigmatic as its author. In this he is outspoken, witty, provocative and sometimes frankly puzzling. Newspaper men love reading it, because Eric, as proprietor, can write things they would never be allowed to themselves.

When his daughter got married in 1982, he told his readers that because of this event he hadn't been able to give his column 'the care and thought it should have, in view of the intelligent appraisal which I am fortunate to receive from readers of *The Cornish Times.*' He added: 'I'm not going to churn out a hack thing, and that is all I could manage for this week.'

I envied him. Writing a regular column myself, I wish I could sometimes say that I can't produce because I've got a hangover, a headache, unexpected visitors or the washing to do. And still expect to get paid.

Journalists speak of Eric among themselves with a mixture of envy and humour. As the proprietor he can write what he likes—barring the laws of libel, but he takes care not to be taken to court, and any 'little misunderstandings' are settled by suitably agreed payments.

His other contributions to the paper consist of regular coverage of the proceedings of the Cornwall County Council. This he does very fully, often in a chatty, Nigel Dempster Diary style, mentioning the hats worn by the lady members or their outfits—those well cut, with 'no buttons or bows' always receiving acclamation. He also writes the Business Intelligence column, which is a mine of useful and offbeat information.

Other events he likes to attend include the annual Royal Cornwall Show, any prestigious openings, or private views of art exhibiti-

Eric Putnam and the staff of ***The Cornish Times.***

While painting his mother, David Jagger did this pencil sketch of the young Eric.

tions. One such happening was the opening of Plymouth's Theatre Royal, attended by Princess Margaret. For this he hired a Daimler limousine, and persuaded the proprietor of the firm to wear a chauffeur's uniform, complete with leather gaiters.

'Then', he wrote in his piece in the paper 'there was The Hitch.' The limousine arrived outside the theatre, but the driver remained resolutely in his seat. Wrote Eric: 'Since the crowd were pressing round, I expressed my view sotto voce. He thereupon got out and opened the stately door. I then cried in a loud voice: "Come back at eleven o'clock James."

'I tell you I reckon I gave a superb performance to the Public, and considerably enlivened a patient Public waiting in the rain. And I was holding a copy of *The Cornish Times.*'

Which rather backs up the comment of the BBC's Sandi Marshall, who after interviewing him for their programme said: 'Shall I tell you what I think about you?' Eric related the episode in his column as follows: ' "Go on!" I replied archly, tapping her on the arm. "I think you are wonderful too!" She gave me a look which put me in my place. Wallop! She continued: "I think you are a showman".'

The businessman in Eric recognises that for a newspaper to prosper you need to be talked about to keep the readers' interest. He used to send 50p to everyone who wrote a letter to the paper—much to their surprise—but now sends them first-day covers or books of stamps.

One of his most successful advertising campaigns was to take space on the backs of buses, with such slogans as 'Read by Kilroy' and 'Peter Pan never bathed'. He is now doing it again, but this time the slogans will all be in Cornish: *Ny a gar Kernow*—We love Cornwall; *Kernow agas Dynargh*—Cornwall welcomes you; and *My a red an termynyow Kernewek*—I read *The Cornish Times.*

In fact he works hard at promoting Cornish things. The firm issues its own calendars in Cornish, the heading on the paper is given in Cornish as well as the date, and he has a sticker of a Cornish flag on the back of his car.

Knowing how much importance the Cornish attach to 'being Cornish' he told me that when he first came to Cornwall he invented an uncle who had important Cornish connections 'a long time ago'. 'If the person I was talking to came from East Cornwall then I said he lived in West Cornwall and vice versa.'

Then one day he found to his astonishment that the story was true—for from America he was sent the family tree of the Puttenhams of Puttenham from 1086 to 1900. And there he found Henry de Puttenham, who was a follower of Edmund Plantagenet, *Earl of Cornwall*, in 1285; and that Alice, who married Sir George Puttenham in the early sixteenth century was an ancestor of the Earls of Plymouth.

'I had the tree from the Putnam family of Salem' says Eric. 'I think they figure in the dreadful witch hunt there—anyway they are named among the hunters in the play *The Witches of Salem.* His coat of arms shows a wolf holding an antler in its mouth, and his family motto is *Nec Metu Nec Dubitatione*—Without Doubt or Fear.

He admits that he has two ambitions. One is to be a guest at a Royal Garden Party in his own right (fulfilled) and the other is to be a Cornish Bard 'wafting around in those blue robe things'.

He puts a lot of effort into getting and keeping his advertisers. When Mike Robertson withdrew his Trago Mills advertisements from the paper in 1982, Eric jokingly referred to this several times in his column. When the Trago ads were resumed, he personally delivered a crate of champagne to Mr Robertson's Spanish style home in Twowatersfoot.

If champagne is his favourite tipple, and smoked salmon his favourite food, Eric believes in the good life in other ways. Hand-tailored suits naturally; Gucci shoes and briefcase; an Alfa Romeo of the most expensive sort; lunch parties for friends, when he will pick up the tab for anything over £100.

But like many rich men he has his own little economies. He likes going to any reception where there is free food and drink; he will never pay to get into an event if he can use his Press pass, and admits that he will always take a handful of the small packets of sugar or milk which are put on cafe tables, one of his favourite eating places, which he often mentions in his column, being the buffet at Truro Station.

Despite a lifetime of good eating—his father owned the famous

Left: Farringdon House, near Exeter, from the park. During the Second World War the top floor housed Polish airmen, who flew from nearby Exeter Airport. Anti-aircraft batteries were in the park, the stables housed the unit, with the NAAFI in the coach-house. The house was later sold to the Ministry of Works, and after the war became a special school for young girls, run by the Home Office.

Below: The Drawing Room: The panelling and the yellow silk panels with flower motifs were looted from the Summer Palace, Peking in 1858/59, during the second war waged there by the British. Two bedrooms were knocked out to get enough height to take the panels.

teashop called Gunters in Mayfair, and his brother the firm which caters for the Lord Mayor's Show—he says he is quite happy with a poached egg on toast or sausage ragout.

Only recently he discovered the Georgian-style shopfront of 'Birch, Birch and Co' in the Flambards village in the Aero Park near Helston was the shop owned by his brother, who is now a lock-keeper at Sonning, near Reading. In the book giving the story of the village, Audrey Hale writes: 'Throughout two centuries Birch's purveyed the viands for civic banquets of the City of London and the majority of the City Companies . . . in 1967 Mr Putnam of the Birch, Birch shop at 3, Angel Court (our shop) presented a decorative crown, which had been on the premises for many years, to the Victoria and Albert Museum.'

His office at the top of the building in Liskeard is more like a page out of *House and Garden.* White chairs in Chinese Chippendale style are grouped round a long table. There are white lamps each side of his large desk, while a tall vase with an art nouveau base contains seasonal flowers. On the wall hangs a large Habitat thermometer next to some of his huge collection of Cornish prints. These number about 500, and cover every wall of the house at Great Place, which is a listed building.

He started collecting them after going into Agnews in London one day and asking for 'a nice thing of Cornwall'. 'Oh', exclaimed the salesman, 'Sir Geoffrey Harmsworth comes here for the same thing.' Eric told me: 'This raised my hackles, and I was determined I would beat Geoffrey at it—and I did.' In a further reference to his 'graphics', he will tell you that they are there 'to identify all at *The Cornish Times* with Cornwall'.

His other collection is much more valuable. It consists of French paintings of the nineteenth and twentieth centuries, which he loves to gaze at for their inherent beauty, although at the same time being very aware of their value.

He was born at Farringdon House, near Exeter. Set in 3,000 acres, the mansion had an indoor staff of fourteen, plus two chauffeurs who looked after 'at least three or four Rolls Royces'. A Home Office school for girls has been housed there for some years.

His father will be remembered for introducing Friesian cattle into Devonshire in the 1920s. 'He brought the Haydon herd from Aylesbury in a special train,' Eric said. 'He was the first to bring them to the county—the local farmers didn't mind, but the Devon cattle breeders and Seal Hayne College took strong objection.'

Eric was educated at Harrow, but he didn't go on to Oxford or Cambridge, which was the usual thing, but went off to the Universities of Berlin and Orleans. As a result his writing and conversation is peppered with French and German phrases. Lady Sayer is 'cette femme' etc . . .

One of his most enterprising schemes, which won him international fame, was to insure every reader of *The Cornish Times* with a firm of Lloyds underwriters for £20,000 'in the event of him/her being killed or injured by falling debris from the skylab after its re-entry into the earth's atmosphere.

Luckily the firm didn't have to pay out!

As *The Cornish Times* reported: 'The gigantic American Columbia Broadcasting Service (CBS) had an American Outside Broadcast crew right in Liskeard, as did the Beeb' to report on the offer.

Eric believes in keeping fit. He starts his day with a twenty-minute yoga session, followed by five minutes of prayers—he is a practising Catholic—using all the Cornish Saints in rotation.

Ask him if he is an eccentric, and he will deny it.

'I just have fun with my money,' he says.

Johnnie Bennett

A tramp by his very lifestyle must be eccentric—for everything he does flies in the face of convention. He doesn't have a home or 'fixed abode', has abandoned his family, spends his time moving from one location to the next, and—more often than not—doesn't know where his next meal is coming from.

But how does one find a tramp to interview, especially when their numbers have dwindled so much they are nearly non-existent?

A letter in the *West Briton*, during their 'Good Neighbour' scheme caught my eye. It was from Mr Johnnie Bennett, aged 76, 'a gentleman of the road', who nominated Mrs Christine Rashleigh of Mount, near Bodmin, for 'all the good work she does for old people'.

I contacted Mrs Rashleigh, and she told me she hadn't seen Johnnie for some time, that he hadn't come in April when he usually did on his way down through Cornwall, or at the end of August on his way back. She was worried that he was ill, or something had happened to him.

I wrote a piece about him in my column in *The Western Morning News* in September, 1982, with the result that Mrs Rashleigh was inundated with telephone calls and letters giving sightings of Johnnie. He was obviously alive and well, and did call in to see her—but by the time I had arranged to get there, he had gone again.

I pieced together Johnnie's story from various people who had befriended him—all incidentally women. Mrs Rashleigh said that Johnnie had told her that he and his sisters were orphaned about the time of the First World War, and they were sent to Australia under the orphans and farmers scheme. Johnnie eventually became an electrician, and lived with his sisters, but because he 'didn't want to be a bloody queer' he left home and began his wanderings. His travels took him to different countries, and he learnt several languages, including French and Aborigine.

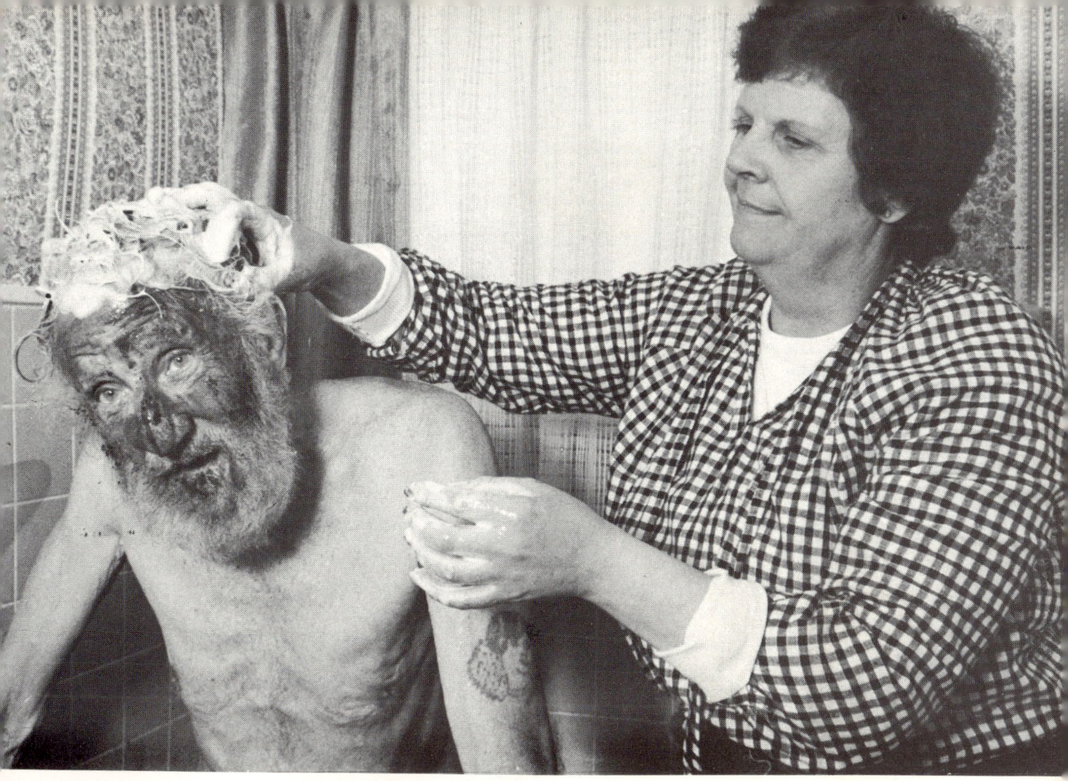

Johnnie Bennett:
'After a hot bath,
he loves to dress up.'

Before taking to the road he had a girl friend in Essex. 'He told me they were going to get married, but he didn't feel he was ready for it,' Christine Rashleigh told me, as we sat together in her cosy caravan home in the woods near Bodmin Moor. 'He left her, intending to go back, but he never did. He talks a lot about her, and says the tattoo on his arm is of her.' And sure enough if you look at the tattoo on his upper left arm in the photograph, there is a pretty girl with Marcel waved hair, framed by a large collar.

Another version of his story is that he went back to South Africa after the Second World War, that he was repatriated from there in 1947, and that was when he met the girl in Essex.

Trying to build up a picture of Johnnie's lifestyle today is equally difficult. I was told that because he originally came from Scotland, he travels back there, making his way through small coastal villages, where he has built up contacts, and where he can also get a swim—something he loves to do.

Others say that nowadays he only covers Devon and Cornwall. At one time after moving from St Ives, where he would pose for the artists, he would make his way to a cave near Mousehole, which he found warm and comfortable. But the land changed hands, he wasn't made welcome by the new owner, and so doesn't go there now.

In the winter he visits a 'very kind lady', a farmer's wife on Dartmoor. The story goes that she has a son at public school, who brings him his meals in the vacations.

I asked Christine Rashleigh how many miles a day Johnnie would cover when he was staying with her.

'He would often walk ten to fifteen miles round here, but I think the most he would do in a day would be about thirty miles. He gets a lift sometimes—but not very often.'

He is usually afraid of the police, she told me. 'If he sees them coming—he's off.' At those times his movements were 'like a greyhound'. Said Christine: 'If he wants to move—he moves!'

Of course that could be difficult if he was weighted down with the usual equipment which he carries. This includes a frying pan, a large saucepan, a big spoon marked 'British Rail', a knife, a mustard tin round his neck for money, and other tins and polythene bags containing food.

He is so used to sleeping rough that when she put a bed down for him, he couldn't sleep, and had to go back to the straw in the chicken shed. He doesn't like being dirty, and will bathe in a stream, a river or the sea whenever he can, and appreciates having a proper bath.

'He often swims in the river here in the nude,' Christine told me.

After a hot bath, he loves to 'dress up'. Said Christine: 'He likes to wear a shirt and a tie with it. He comes up here for a meal—his table manners are perfect—and he will often give me flowers afterwards.' She reflected: 'In fact he's the only man who gives me flowers.'

He knew about different sorts of food, having worked in a hotel at one time. 'I gave him cheesecake one day, and he said it was delicious, and he hadn't had it for a long time.'

Obviously, however, scavenging for food was ingrained in him, because she was horrified one day, after having given him a good meal, to see his hand come round the door to take the dog's food from its bowl!

Any food he has been given—perishable things like butter and milk—he will store in biscuit tins, tied in polythene bags and place them in the river. When he is on the road he will catch a stray pigeon, cook hedgehogs in clay—or, when really desperate—exist on berries from the hedgerow. Mrs Jill Newton, wife of the artist, David Newton, of St Keverne—said they had been amazed at the initiative he showed in obtaining food in the wild.

'He would trap birds, or stalk an injured pigeon, and look in the gardens of derelict cottages for root vegetables, potatoes or apples. He was always thrilled when given a mackerel—but reckoned that farmers were more generous than fishermen.'

Jill said he told her that he liked the freedom of his life, and the feeling of being close to nature. 'People don't know how wonderful it is to walk through woods in the early morning,' he told her. If it's dark, a sixth sense will tell him if there is a branch, hole or bank to be avoided. 'It's a gift everyone has, but most have lost,' he said.

Jill thinks he is 'a very intelligent man, a real character.' She added: 'He is very well abreast of what's happening in the world. He likes to read a newspaper, and he's a super person to have a conversation with.'

While he was with them in the spring, her husband painted his portrait, and this was included in an exhibition at the Falmouth Art Gallery later in the year.

Another woman who has befriended him is Mrs T.A. Satchwell, who lives in the Feock area. One day she was practising her recorder in a meadow, when Johnnie's bearded face appeared at the gate.

'He said the sound he had heard reminded him of a Greek shepherd playing on his pipes.' Later he told her 'how nice it would be' if he had a little pipe to play. 'I got him a small flageolet—but I think someone took it from him.'

Why does Johnnie Bennett live the way he does?

I wasn't able to ask him that question myself, but Christine Rashleigh told me that he had originally 'wanted to do what he wanted'. This seems to fit my definition of an eccentric—someone who does what he wants, despite convention.

Many of us perhaps envy the complete independence of a tramp like Johnnie—but how many could endure the hardships, hunger and harrassment which goes with it?

Sean Dorman: 'Aged 71 and he hasn't been to a doctor for fifty years.'

Sean Dorman

A man who does eighty deep knee-bends on Mondays, Thursdays and Saturdays at the age of 71, while doing his housework, is certainly to be admired—although some might consider it eccentric.

But this is only one outward sign of Sean Dorman's keen interest in matters connected with health. He also uses a chest expander every day, except Sunday; does exercises in his bath on Tuesdays and Fridays, which were devised by the Italian proprietor of a hotel in London's Shaftesbury Avenue; keeps to a strict vegetarian diet and fasts for 24 hours twice a month.

He hasn't been to a doctor for fifty years and, at an age when most people would have long since retired, he works a week of over fifty hours. He runs a manuscript criticism agency, edits and produces a quarterly magazine of his own creation, both of which activities barely cover their cost, as well as writing his own novels and putting his early work in book form.

His French ancestors, the de Dormans, include a Count who was founder of the College of Beauvais, a Chancellor of France, an Archbishop, a Bishop, an Ambassador to the Pope and a Steward of the King.

His Irish uncle, Dr Lennox Robinson, one of the directors of the famous Abbey Theatre in Dublin, once kicked him up the backside, with T.S. Eliot watching from behind a door; he interviewed the Aga Khan who, at the time, was lying on a bed in the Ritz Hotel in Paris; when he was a schoolmaster, he lived in a tent, which he had devised to withstand gales of 70 mph, and whenever he goes abroad, he spends his time jaunting in cable cars.

Sean, a tall, balding man with glasses and a beard, met me wearing a brown Aran sweater as I searched for his house in the narrow, delightful streets near the church in Fowey. The tiny, blue-painted cottage with iron grilles over its lower windows, which he copied from Buckingham Palace, is named Raffeen, after his family home in Ireland.

It is here, without any help since his wife died, and without the benefit of a telephone, that he lives a solitary existence, surrounded by his collection of clocks, carrying out the numerous tasks connected with the thing he likes doing best—writing. For, from the age of fourteen, when he won a prize as the best prose writer in his first term at his public school—St Columba's College, near Dublin—writing for him has come 'first, second—and third'.

But, as everyone knows, getting your work published can be a matter of luck—and more often heartbreak. Some writers use an agent, others send directly to publishers and wait for the rejection slips, others again use the 'vanity press' and pay for their material to appear in print.

Sean Dorman has gone one better. He decided to do the whole job himself on a cottage industry basis—from typing the pages of his books and his quarterly journal *Writing*, with a circulation of about 300, through the processes of duplicating, collating, stapling and binding. He then addresses all the envelopes for the journal subscribers, stamps and posts them.

The journal—a 6½″ x 8″ format—contains poems, letters and articles about writing, but is currently mainly devoted to a serialisation of his book *Valley of Graneen.* Another book of reminiscences about his life in Ireland, *Limelight Over The Liffey*, has already appeared in this form. It also contains advertisements for the Sean Dorman Manuscript Society, a notice to advertisers recommending the magazine, a subscription form for the magazine and an advertisement on the back cover for his son's restaurant at Newquay.

Despite having written a successful novel, which was recommended by the Book Society; edited or ghost written six non-fiction books, including one on the Aga Khan's horses, co-translated a German novel for Putnams, the London publishers; had a burlesque staged by the Dublin Gate Theatre; and a radio play and short stories broadcast on the BBC and Radio Eireann, he still feels the need for a sounding board for his work and the criticism of fellow writers.

This is the main reason why he runs his literary agency. It used to have ninety members from different parts of the world, but now is 'held down by force' to not more than 35 members, resident in the United Kingdom.

'I need the criticism for my own work, and I have the secondary pleasure of the companionship,' he explains. He puts it 'in the wringer' by circulating it with the others, and is prepared to cut and alter anything 'a hundred times if necessary'.

Some might say this was a very elaborate and time-consuming way of receiving criticism, but Sean's whole house is centred round this activity. In one room he has an IBM electric typewriter with proportional spacing, on which the text is produced. There is also an electronic scanner, for cutting stencils, and a duplicating machine. Art work pages are made from paste-ups.

Wooden vegetable racks, treated with caustic soda and one coat of varnish to bring up the grain, hold completed pages of the magazine, with flower pots sitting incongruously on top. A metal-banded sea chest in the dining room contains a book binder, and a five feet tall metal rack of shelving holds the completed sheets of his book.

He used the redundancy money he received, after a school where he was teaching closed down, to pay for the first year's instalment on printing equipment.

When I called he was working on a chapter of *Limelight over the*

Sean in his kaftan amongst his modern equipment.

Liffey. He plans to print a private edition of just over 200 copies 'exactly as I want, without anyone else interfering'. To get a professional finish to the page, he has to make sure the right hand margin is straight, or 'justified' as they say in the trade. It's a slow, tedious job. He types two thirds of a line in the usual way. Then, after counting all the spaces for the rest of the line, works backwards from the right-hand margin. This operation is made more difficult because of the different number of spaces taken up by certain letters. Most letters take three spaces, as do figures and double quotes. A few narrow letters like i, l, j and f take two. Most capitals, and the letter w, take four. An m takes five, while most punctuation takes only one. He has to remember all this as he types the last piece of the line backwards, polishing the English too as he goes!

'Alas, I can't afford a self-justifying typewriter,' he says.

He has got five books planned, and he works on these between producing his magazine and attending to the circulators. He runs four of these, while his co-director runs two technical ones, and he has a waiting list if anyone drops out. If he had more circulators, it would just mean more work for him, he says. There is a six months trial period for anyone who joins, which costs only £2, while the full subscription is a modest £3.

Comments from those taking part are fulsome. One was pleasantly surprised to find that it wasn't people 'passing round dog-eared manuscripts on which other people wrote crabby comments'. Others say they are 'pleased', 'impressed by the way it is run', 'thrilled', 'simply splendid', 'passed all expectations'—and one commented that he had gone 'from success to success, mainly due to you'.

Several have remarked on the fact that the society is obviously not run as a money-making venture. Sean agrees with this summing up, and says that for the sort of painstaking criticism he gives, a School of Writing would charge £100.

Sean has been a health fanatic from an early age. In his twenties he drank first-pressing olive oil—bought in bulk direct from a Liverpool importer—to increase his weight; lifted dumb-bells and pulled at a chest expander.

He gave me a run-down of his present system.

'On Mondays, Thursdays and Saturdays I do deep knee-bends in the mornings, not only to maintain strength in the legs, but also to keep a good sense of balance.'

To make the routine less tedious he likes to split it up.

'Since I must "do" for myself, clean the house, shop and so on, and since this cottage is three up and three down, with etceteras, i.e. eight living spaces, I do ten of my deep knee bends, and then tidy and/or clean up one living space. So by the time I have done the house, I've done eighty deep knee bends. In addition, I do fifteen exercises without apparatus, for all parts of the body. While I'm doing the exercises, I'm also talking to my language machine, in French or German.

'On Tuesdays and Fridays I do a system of exercises in the bath for the face, arms, legs, waist and abdomen. They also prevent high blood pressure developing. I have Epsom salts in the water to draw out waste toxins through the skin. I finish up by massaging with cold cream. Every morning before getting out of bed I do exercises for the eyes, face, neck, abdomen, hands and wrists.

'On Wednesday mornings I do no exercises as I bus into St Austell for shopping. Every afternoon or evening, Monday to Saturday inclusive, I do exercises with an expander. As I can only afford a certain amount of time, I split them up into a rota system. One week I do ten exercises for the smallest muscles with one steel spring strand on the expander, each exercise ten times. The next week I do eleven exercises for larger muscles with two strands on the expander. The third week I do six exercises for the largest muscles with three strands on the expander. Always ten times each. The fourth week, I'm back to one strand again, and so forth. I am pulling and pushing the same poundages now as I did in my twenties.'

Obviously Sean is a man who really needs to know what day of the week it is.

I also asked him about his diet.

'Except for Wednesdays, when I'm in St Austell, my diet is—Breakfast, one large slice of stone-ground brown bread, with "Outline" margarine, which is 50% water, and honey.'

Sean took an immense interest in the piece I was writing about him, and sent me fifteen postcards and letters after I had seen him. One card said: 'In order to shift my diet even further towards eating as much of it raw as possible,' he had given up stone-ground bread, Outline and honey for breakfast, and instead 'just had some dates'. He pointed out that this 'gets rid of the salt in the bread and the fats in the Outline'.

Lunch is five pieces of Ryvita and a glass of pure, unsweetened apple juice. Tea—an apple. Supper—turn about, day by day: either potato, carrot and onion boiled in water, which was taken first as soup because it contained all the mineral salts from the vegetables; or a salad of lettuce, pieces of tomato and cucumber, teaspoonfuls of cottage cheese, a cut-up hard-boiled egg with a dressing made of cider vinegar, vegetable oil and egg. This was followed by natural yoghurt, sweetened with rose-hip syrup, and a small glass of raw carrot or beetroot juice.

He told me that later in the evening—he goes to bed late, between 1 am and 2 am—he has a small bowl of porridge with a teaspoonful of crude black cane molasses and a little milk mixed into it; and still later a small bowl of long-grain brown rice with a little dark brown sugar. Later again, he will have a small bowl of muesli with a little milk.

'When I go to bed, I have a couple of bananas—so filling, so easily

On Sean's table a week's supply of tablets and food.

digested, they put me to sleep faster than any bedtime drink.'

Before each of his three main meals he has a teaspoon of cider vinegar in a little warm water to augment the gastric juices, which, he says, tend to diminish with age; two garlic perles as a blood thinner, a Vitamin E capsule as an oxygenator, three Brewers Yeast tablets for proteins, an aquatone capsule against arthritis, a teaspoonful of sunflower seed oil and a Vitamin C tablet.

He starts each day with a Vitamin A, Vitamin B12 and a Ginseng capsule, helped down with a spoonful of Ribena. Each month he has two 24-hour fasts from solid food.

He doesn't smoke, doesn't normally drink tea or coffee, never eats salt and is 'very near' to being a non-drinker of alcohol.

He told me that he first started to get work published in health magazines from 1936 onwards—such publications as *Health and Strength, Health and Efficiency, Superman, New Health, Health for All, Armchair Science* and *Sunbathing Review*, specialising in articles on sunbathing, sun lamps—both carbon-arc and mercury vapour—and infra-red lamps.

Most of his information, he confided, came from sun lamp brochures, and he would get a guinea a thousand words for articles such as 'Help Yourself to Sunshine', 'Re-Stock Yourself With Sunshine' and 'Sunbathing In The Home'. When we first talked, he jokingly referred to these as his 'Ultra-Violet Period' and his 'Infra-Red Period', mocking his youthful efforts by referring to them as Picasso did to his Blue Period.

He has always been keen on sunbathing, and when he designed the tent he lived in as a schoolmaster, which consisted of an outer tent 16 feet long, 12 feet wide and 7½ feet high, with a smaller tent inside, he had flaps in the roofs of both tents, which allowed him to sunbathe, or to sleep under the stars.

At home he may often be seen wandering round the house in summer in a kaftan, made by his younger daughter, Madeleine, who is a graduate of the University of Exeter. His elder daughter, Edwina, is a graduate of the University of Kent, holds the Diploma of the Rose Bruford College of Speech and Drama, and works in the theatre in London, mainly in mime.

'The kaftan was made for me to use when sunbathing in the courtyard, being easy to open when the sun is out, and to close when, the next moment, it goes in,' Sean told me.

In his rather dark sitting-room, mysteriously lit by red-shaded lamps, and crowded with books, paintings and drawings, he showed me his family tree, which hangs impressively above his desk. It is in two parts, because although they are a Protestant, Anglo-Irish family, their ancestry dates back to fourteenth-century France before the Reformation. That part of the tree was recorded by his uncle, the Venerable Hobart Dorman, Archdeacon of Cloyne and father of E.H.H. (Ted) Dorman, who was Chairman of the St Austell Urban District Council from 1964 to 1966, an Alderman of the St Austell with Fowey Borough Council, a former Cornwall County Councillor (1963 to 1981) and Chairman of the Education Committee (1977 to 1981). The earlier French section ends with Suzanne de Dormans, who married Francoise de St Basseu, Lord of Berlize and Steward of the King, who died in 1638.

The de Dormans became Protestants after the Reformation, and joined the Huguenots, who were persecuted and massacred. This became so bad in the seventeenth century that over half a million people fled from France to Protestant countries like Prussia and England. Some of the de Dormans came to County Cork in Ireland—a mainly Catholic country, but Protestant dominated, where they would have been welcomed by the all-powerful Anglo-Irish minority, who ruled with the backing of London.

The first ancestor recorded in County Cork is Richard Dorman of Monygormy, who was born around 1670 and died in 1749. There is obviously not a very great gap between the death of Suzanne de Dormans in 1638 and the birth of Richard Dorman in about 1670, but Sean told me that because his great uncle, the Venerable Hobart Dorman, had not one hundred per cent established the connection between the de Dormans and the Dormans, the College of Heralds would only permit him to use the coat of arms of the de Dormans provided he added fleur-de-lys.

So the family coat of arms includes a shield with three lions' heads against a background of fleur-de-lys, with the motto *In Arduis Viget Virtus.* After some thought, and communication with his cousin Ted at Pentewan, who is an ex-headmaster, Sean decided this could be translated as 'Under difficulties valour increases.'

Sean's father was the Chief Engineer, Roads and Buildings, of the Punjab in India, and an ex-officio member of the Punjab Government. His mother wrote short stories and articles for Indian and Irish periodicals; a children's book and, as part author with her brothers Tom and Lennox Robinson, a book of reminiscences, both

The Dorman family's coat of arms includes a shield with three lions' heads.

published in London, as well as radio plays for Radio Eireann.

Sean was born in Cork, and was taken to India by his family when he was a few weeks' old. He returned to Ireland when he was eight, with his parents and two sisters. When they went back to India, he was boarded at Castle Park preparatory school at Dalkey, now a suburb of Dublin.

He there came into contact with his famous and colourful godfather—his uncle, Dr Lennox Robinson. He was the author of *The Whiteheaded Boy* and many other plays performed throughout the English-speaking world; he edited *The Oxford Book of Irish Verse* and was at the centre, through his directorship of the Abbey Theatre, of the Irish literary movement, led by W.B. Yeats, Lady Gregory, George Moore, Sean O'Casey and George Bernard Shaw.

Sean remembers him as being 'immensely tall, immensely thin, Bohemian and celebrated'. He introduced Sean to glamorous theatrical people and others—including Yeats, O'Casey and Barry Fitzgerald. Through his own magazine *Commentary* Sean came into contact with such visitors from England as John Betjeman, Laurence Olivier, Sybil Thorndike and Deborah Kerr.

At the age of ten or eleven, he was taken on the back of his uncle's motor bike. 'I felt the incongruousness of this utterly unmechanical man, in his floppy, eccentric clothes, bow tie and very broad-brimmed hat, guiding a machine.'

His uncle took him to see his own plays at the Abbey Theatre, when he would 'laugh with unrestrained enjoyment' at his own jokes—even though, comments Sean, he must have heard them at least twenty times before.

And when he was put in charge of buying Sean's wardrobe for Oxford, he did this on an extravagant scale, buying him four hats when he never wore one, and a dozen or more white waistcoats when two or three would have been enough.

After Sean came down from Oxford, it was decided he must be set up as a writer. His uncle gave him a batch of introductions to various celebrated authors, including E.M. Forster. Forster gave him a large plate of cherries, and an article of his in *The New Statesman* to read. When Sean admired the construction, he replied that it was 'like putting together a soufflé'.

But eventually his uncle began to drink too much, and a love-hate relationship developed between them, culminating in the kick in the stern given by his uncle, who had hidden behind his drawing-room door, with his wife—the artist, Dolly Travers—and T.S. Eliot.

Writing about the incident in his book *Limelight Over the Liffey*, Sean says: 'Knowing him, I realised that he had organised the business under the guise of a joke; but the strength of that kick also told me that there was no laughter in his heart. As I passed a small table, I saw a manuscript on it. Supposing it to be my uncle's I picked it up and dropped it on the floor—also under the guise of a joke.'

As he went up the garden path, he heard his aunt's voice behind him, and suddenly realised that the typescript—a very thick one—was nice, courteous T.S. Eliot's lecture for the Abbey Theatre.

Despite the help of a clergyman and psychiatrist, his uncle was not able to overcome his alcoholism, but this did not prevent the University of Dublin conferring a Doctorate of Literature on him, and when he died he was given a national funeral, with burial at St Patrick's Cathedral.

His other godfather could not have been more different. He was Surgeon General John Cotter Dorman, CMG, who was in the Medical Corps of the British Army. He lived an extremely long life at Rampart House, Kinsale, County Cork, and in his youth was a fine athlete—rowing for Dublin University at Henley.

In the summer holidays, when most of the Dormans tended to gather in the ancient little seaside town of Kinsale, some twenty miles from Cork city, two tennis afternoons a week were held for the Anglo-Irish gentry. The first, known as the 'practice' afternoon, took place at the home of Sean's branch of the family, Raffeen, after which his own cottage is named. The 'real' tennis afternoon was held later in the week at Rampart House.

General Dorman's distinguished military family include his son and son-in-law, both of whom eventually commanded regiments. His son-in-law (married to his younger daughter, Marcia) was General Sir Walter Venning. He was Col. of the Duke of Cornwall's Light Infantry from 1935 to 1947; the founder and Col. Commandant of the Royal Electrical and Mechanical Engineers; Director of Movement and Quartering at the War Office before the 2nd World War and Quartermaster General of the forces in that war. Added to that he was Aide-de-Camp General to King George VI.

Sean's cousin, Brig. Edward Dorman, commanded the 4th/7th Royal Irish Dragoon Guards, as well as a cavalry brigade; the Yorkshire Home Guard in 1940 and was Assistant Chief Constable of the War Dept. Constabulary from 1944 to 1946.

The Brigadier's son now lives near Cork, while General Venning's son lives in Plymouth.

One wonders what influences Sean's very different godfathers had on him.

On the surface, the literary and Bohemian lifestyle of his uncle Lennox might seem to have won the day, but the rigid regime Sean has instituted as far as his diet, exercise and health are concerned might be said to have a very military flavour.

A paradox, a paradox, a most ingenious paradox, as Gilbert would have said . . . but perhaps the making of an eccentric?

René Halkett

René Halkett died on March 7, 1983, and four days later he was buried near the walls of the fifteenth-century church of St Julitta at Lanteglos-by-Camelford.

Ian Fell, a former producer with Mid-day Parade, BBC, Plymouth, in his tribute spoke of René's genius; how he 'approached every challenge with passion and remarkable skill, and was a stickler for getting things precisely right'.

Not long before his death, he wrote about himself as follows:

René Halkett, born 5 February, 1900 was a member of the Stagecraft Workshop of the original Bauhaus in Weimar.

According to the published aims of this revolutionary institution, one would have expected a number of craft-masters training apprentices to become masters of the various crafts connected with the stage. In fact there was not even one master of a practical craft.

But, as a whole, the Bauhaus seemed to be the liveliest, most stimulating place in the chaotic, artistic world after the First World War, and Halkett left it under the influence of Feininger and Klee before the Bauhaus moved to Dessau.

Halkett says of himself—'I became a painter, a perpetual journeyman of life, travelling from one country to another, observing and absorbing all that this amazing century has to offer.'

From childhood on, the end of the journey seemed predestined—but he felt he could only find it in England, so some years before the Second World War he moved, with his wife, to London, and then to Devonshire.

A brief and uneventful period of service in the Army was followed by what he calls 'a variety of weird, war-connected occupations', like moving to the Special Operations Directorate, and after the war to different assignments. For two years he was a research analyst at the US War Crimes Trials.

René Halkett: He 'approached every challenge with passion and remarkable skill'.

R.H. 48

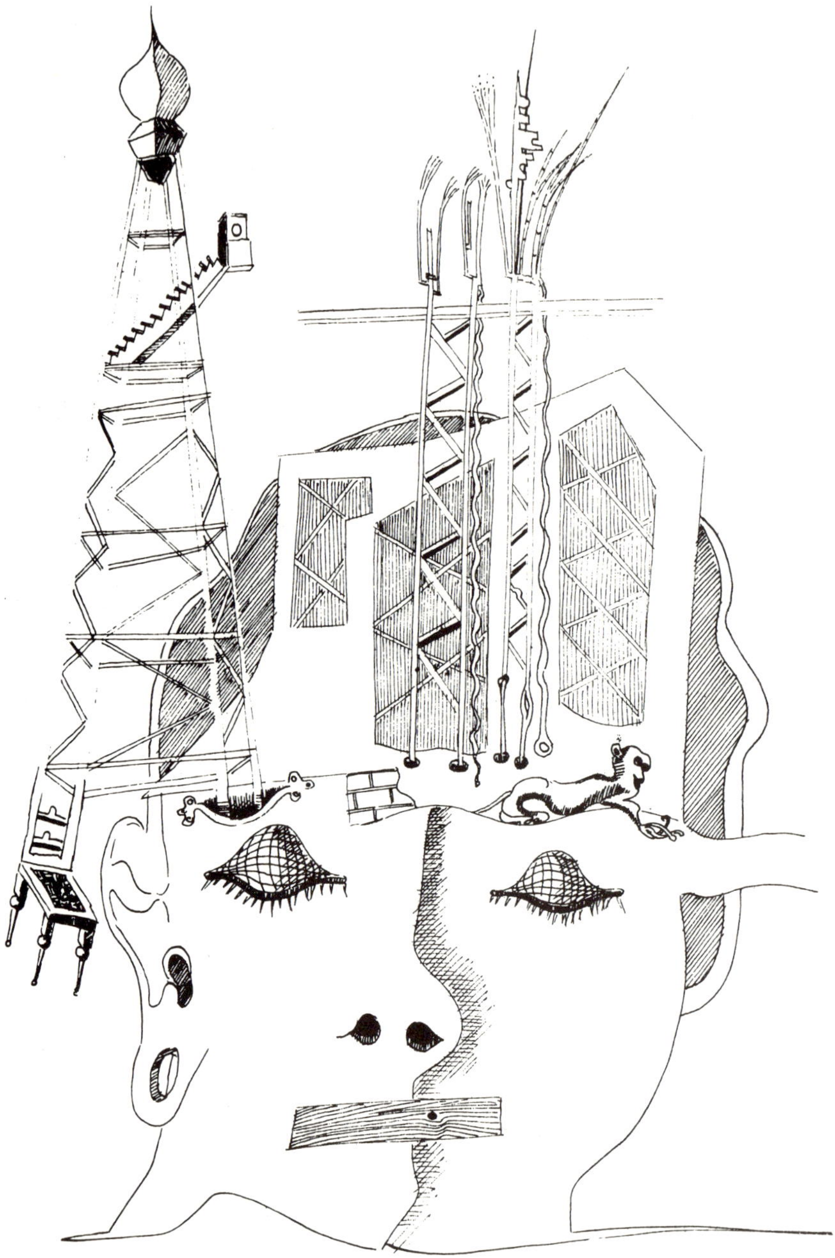

In all these occupations painting was out of the question, and the result was a strictly limited collection of drawings, which only two years ago were exhibited and published.

Halkett had never been interested in drawing, possibly because of an experience in early childhood.

The drawings, which a teacher had discovered on the empty pages of the boy's exercise books, made him pay a solemn visit to his pupil's parents, warning them that the 'incoherent and un-natural figures' could only indicate a deranged mind.

The parents were secretly amused—but in order to stop damaging gossip in the school, the boy was taken to be seen by the eminent psychiatrist, Otto Binswanger, who attested in writing that René was 'an intelligent and lively youngster and mentally perfectly normal'.

René says: 'I wish I could have that paper now!'

For sixteen years Halkett lived in a cottage in Cornwall, where he 'at long last felt properly at home', and worked as a painter, broadcaster and lecturer.

In 1980 he added still another to his many activities—he discovered the Northampton based group 'bauhaus' and recorded two of his poems 'Nothing' and 'Armour', with the then 23-year-old David Jay providing the supporting music.

Apparently no generation gap here!

Two Eccentrics

Two clerics in West Cornwall earlier this century, who were friends, could certainly be described as eccentrics.

They were the Rev. Bernard Walke of St Hilary, whose eccentricity was of the unconventional, artistic sort and the Rev. Sandys Wason of Cury—who was, in my view, a genuine eccentric.

Both preferred to be called 'Father', and were very High Church. This led to Wason being deprived of his living and thrown out of his vicarage, and to Walke having his church desecrated, while being held prisoner inside.

Bernard Walke, known to his friends as 'Ber', wore a long, black cloak, a hat like a Spanish sombrero, and rode about in a donkey shay.

In his time at St Hilary, near Marazion, he was accused of being a German spy; was involved in a pitched battle in a public hall in Penzance when he had a curtain thrown over his head; helped to re-open a mine; turned a pub into a children's home and became nationally famous for his nativity play, broadcast from the church.

Before coming to St Hilary, when he lived at Polruan, he had on several occasions signed on in tramp steamers, carrying china clay to Spain, and before that he was a curate in St Ives.

Later he became the friend of such internationally known writers and artists as Walter De la Mere, Compton Mackenzie, A.J. Munnings, Laura Knight and Lamorna Birch.

In his book *Twenty Years at St. Hilary* Bernard Walke says: 'We had already begun to attract the queer people with whom it has been our lot to be associated during the whole of these 20 years.'

◂The painting of St Joan by Anne Walke in St Hilary Church with the carved wooden French statue of St Anne.

Some arrived on the strength of being spoken to in a train, others were sent by friends, but for the most part 'they are people who have drifted in as the birds drift westwards in a hard winter, or have landed here by mistake.'

But it was his Catholicism which certainly made him talked about at first, and was to prove cataclysmic.

He knew that his parishioners did not want anything different from what they 'belonged to have', but believing that the Catholic movement in the Church of England could have 'no other end but a corporate union with the Apostolic See of Rome', he pressed ahead with the Catholic form of worship, which included the Mass, the accompaniment of the priest at the altar by a small boy who knelt at his side, the ringing of a bell during the offering of the sacrament, the swinging of the censer and much bowing and crossing before the altar.

The church was crowded on the first Sundays after he became vicar, mainly with people from miles around who were curious about the 'play acting' and 'games' which they had heard about.

After the service they stood about in the churchyard, 'and however friendly they might have been during the week in their homes or in the fields, none would speak—all faces would be turned away until I had passed, when there would be laughter and someone would shout "There goes the old Roman Catholic".'

But he never quarrelled with them, and his summing up of their attitude was: 'The parson isn't a bad old sort. We don't dislike he, but we don't altogether hold with his goings on.'

His 'goings on' included introducing into the church six altars, built by local stone-masons; paintings on the front of the choir stalls, describing the lives of Cornish saints, by such artists as Dod Proctor, Ernest Proctor, Norman Garstin, Alathea Garstin and his wife, Anne Walke; in the two side aisles altar pieces of St Joan by his wife and St Francis by Roger Fry, and paintings by a child of ten on the screen of the Lady Chapel.

He gave these chapels and altars names like Altar of the Holy Souls and Chapel of the Sacred Heart and bought statues, such as

The Rev. Curson, Rector of St Hilary, points to the Venetian bracket, supporting the statue of St Joseph, which was dug out of the wall by the Kensitites. ▶

Lis Escop,
Truro.

an early carved wooden figure of St Anne and a flamboyant figure of St Joseph, the work of a Spanish artist of the seventeenth century.

These ornaments, and the introduction of Tabernacles, the Stations of the Cross, a Sanctus bell, candlesticks and a blue votive lamp were to be his final undoing, because it was said they had been brought in 'without faculty'.

At one stage the Bishop of Truro held a public visitation in the church, when he condemned many of the Catholic practices, and he pressed Walke to abandon certain services.

Finally in 1932 Miss Marian King, a parishioner, with two others, obtained judgment in the Consistory Court to remove a number of articles from the church.

Bernard Walke would not accept its judgment, refused to attend its proceedings and was pursued with writs.

Came the day when two motor coaches and two motor cars arrived from Plymouth. They contained members of the Protestant Truth Society, led by Mr J.A. Kensit.

With the aid of crow bars and tools they forced their way into the church, tore down the reredos, designed by Ernest Proctor, at the back of the altar, smashed the fifteenth-century font, dug out a Venetian bracket from the wall supporting the statue of St Joseph and removed the figures of the Virgin Mary and St Anne.

Bernard Walke, a bell ringer and another man were imprisoned in the Chapel of Our Lady. Eventually the Vicar was allowed to take the Sacrament from a tabernacle in the Chapel of the Sacred Heart.

The story, which broke in the national press the next day, brought crowds of sightseers to the church and hundreds of letters of sympathy, many containing gifts of money as well as small sums towards the restoration. Those who saw the interior of the church, with granite blocks dislodged, flowers strewn over the floor and pieces of splintered wood and plaster everywhere, wept openly.

Walke commented: 'I have been in this all my life, and I have got accustomed to it', adding that his grandfather was the Rector of Falmouth 'and exactly the same thing went on there', and that his father was the Vicar of St Peter's, Plymouth, 'so I have two generations behind me.'

◀ A cartoon drawn by the Bishop of Truro's son when Miss King obtained her judgment in the Court.

Left: The main altar, now re-erected in memory of Bernard Walke. St Hilary is depicted in the centre panel of the stained glass window.

Below: The stone altar in the Lady Chapel reinstated in 1983 after lying in pieces in the churchyard. The painting of the Visitation is by Ernest Proctor. The banner shows early embroidery by the nuns of the Convent of the Epiphany in Truro.

A few months later strange motors again arrived. They carried people who sang hymns against the singing of the congregation, and created such a disturbance that no word of the service could be heard. The police came and took the names of those present—some of whom were committed under an order from the Court of the King's Bench.

The ironic sequel to this story is that the same Miss King who was one of the instigators of the desecration of the church, and who had been told by the Bishop, Dr Frere, that she should repent for the part she had played 'in this scandalous business', died in St Michael's Hospital, Hayle in 1955, nursed by Roman Catholic nuns.

On the last day of February, 1983, with clear sunshine still struggling against the holds of winter, I called in at St Hilary Church. At first I thought the way was barred—it was late afternoon, the door must be locked and my mission fruitless.

But as I looked at the church notices in the porch, searching to establish a link with Bernard Walke, the door slowly opened.

'You didn't turn the handle far enough,' said a large, portly, grey-haired figure, who identified himself as the Rev. J. Desmond Curson—'my first name is James, but I never use it'. He had only been installed as Rector the previous Tuesday.

Recognising that my luck was in, I swiftly followed up with: 'Do many people come to St Hilary because of Bernard Walke's book?'

'It's difficult to say,' he said, but in answer to my further enquiry about what was to be seen from the desecration of the church in the 1930s, he told me: 'There are lots of bits left.'

Quickly he gave me a guided tour. His tea was waiting, he explained, and as his wife is partially sighted, I could quite understand why he wanted to get back to her.

Together we looked at the painting by Anne Walke to the left of the south door. 'That wasn't originally here,' said the Rector. 'It was in St Clare and given to us in the last five years.' Another painting by Anne Walke is of St Joan. The bare-headed figure is clad dramatically in shining armour and a white over-mantel. It is a composition in white, grey and silver—more pious than militant.

'Edna Waters Coward could have helped you—she wrote *The Church on The Hill*' says the Rector, 'but her funeral is tomorrow.' At first I thought he meant in the church—but we establish it is in Stourbridge, and I am struck by the coincidence.

'What sort of church are you?' I fumble for words. 'I mean how high do you go?' I added, rather courageously, I thought.

'As high as you can go' he answers. 'I have never made any secret of where I stand. It was the way I was brought up. I didn't know anything else.'

I ask him about the Stations of the Cross, which I see on the walls.

'The Stations were lost, but the crosses were left' he says. 'The Stations were only put back recently.'

As we look back at the altar to the left of the entrance door, the Rector says: 'It was St Michael's in Walke's time. The table under it was found in the church rooms, where they were pouring tea on it.'

Seeing me make a note, he quails visibly. 'I don't think you ought to say that—it would be thought sacrilege of the first order—an indictable offence.'

Later he returned to the subject, and I ask if I may pass it with the Bishop, but he shakes his head. 'It's the Archdeacon one has to contend with—he is the Law Officer.' He hesitates: 'Well, I don't think it would matter.'

Obviously the subject is a very sensitive one in a church with St Hilary's history.

We had reached the chapel to the right of the main altar. The early carved wooden statue of St Anne, riddled with woodworm, but still retaining traces of the original colours, 'is fifteenth-century French' says Mr Curson, 'probably Breton.' St Anne's hand supports a piece of wood like an open book. 'It's where she would be supporting Our Lord and Our Lady' he explains.

And nearby is the statue of St Joseph—the very one which Bernard Walke describes buying in his book, after many visits to a London dealer. It is seventeenth-century Spanish—a lovely thing in a rich, deep gold, the cloak of the saint flaring in realistic and eye-catching folds. It stands on a Venetian bracket, which was dug out of the wall by the Kensitites.

'I'm afraid we haven't been able to put it back properly yet,' said the Rector, pointing to the rather crude support. 'It needs re-assembling.'

'What do you call this chapel?' I asked.

'Well, it's really the Chapel of the Sacred Heart of Jesus, but I call it St Joseph's Chapel—it avoids criticism and a lot of fuss and trouble.'

Behind the altar is the reredos—an edifice in stone of towers and rooms like a fairy palace. The painting in the centre is ascribed to a fifteenth-century artist, Quentin Matsys.

The choir stalls, painted by the Newlyn artists, including Ernest and Dod Proctor, Gladys Hughes and Harold Knight ARA, show St Hilary in a green gown; St Paul with St Michael's Mount in the background and St Senen—an old man lies asleep under a tree and is blessed by a Bishop.

On the screen the other side of the Chancel are the naive paintings in bright colours by Joan Manning Sanders, as fresh and clear as when she painted them as a child.

The Cornish granite altar, with its simple wedge-shaped supports, was consecrated in 1978 as a memorial to Bernard Walke, vicar from 1912 to 1936.

Painted in the panels of the pulpit are legends of St Neot, St Kevin and St Mawes by Ernest Proctor.

In the Lady Chapel the stone altar has just been reinstated. 'It

The reredos in St Joseph's Chapel, representing the City of God, suffered at the hands of the desecraters.

was found in the churchyard and had obviously been thrown there at the time of the desecration' says Mr Curson. 'You can see it's right, because we have matched up the crosses.' I see what he means when he points out the identical shaped crosses on the front of the altar, linking up with a separate stone at the back, which also has crosses on it. The painting of the Visitation in the centre is again by Ernest Proctor.

Next we looked at the commanding light wood carving of Christ on the crucifix on the north wall, the work of Phyllis Yglesias of Mousehole—a memorial to Canon Rogers of Truro Cathedral, who died in the parish in 1928, and one of the articles named in the Faculty Petition.

Round the corner, where there used to be an altar to St Francis, hangs the painting of the saint by Roger Fry.

'I'm afraid I don't like it—I can't arouse any enthusiasm for it,' says the Rector. 'In fact, I think it's horrible.' I have to admit, as I gaze at the gaunt figure of St Francis in its gloomy colours, that I can't help agreeing with him.

Just past this, work was being done on a handsome carved stone niche, which is usually occupied by a statue of the Virgin Mary, and is a memorial to those who took the services following the despoiling of the church.

I explain my presence to the Rector. I also asked him about Wason, and he confirms that Father Wason (pronounced Wayson) was certainly a charming, but eccentric, priest. He ended up in St Julian's Newport in Monmouthshire, he says.

Mr Curson's link with him was that when he lived in Northolt, the Rector of his church was the curate at St Julian's and knew Mr Wason.

His link with Bernard Walke was that his godmother, Helen, who married a Cornishman named Ludlam, knew Walke when he made his London preaching tours.

'They lost their own son called Desmond, so I was called Desmond after him.'

By now I was anxious that the Rector should not miss his tea, but I wanted to look at the paintings, statues and works of art in the church more closely.

'I think I can trust you,' said the Rector, as he shut the south door which, much to my interest, he fastened with a crude piece of wood, explaining that the key was lost.

He showed me where to put the lights out, and the door I should pull to after me, and as we stood outside for a moment, he pointed out the Vicarage, where the Walkes had lived, with Annie's studio, standing high in its gabled tower above the house.

Alone in the church, it was hard not to imagine the scenes of desecration fifty years ago, with the Rector imprisoned in his own church, as the mob went about its ungodly work, smashing and laying waste.

Today all is calm, thanks to the Friends of St Hilary, who in the 1970s did much restoration work.

I threw the switch, which plunged the church into gloom, apart from the single light of the lamp to the right of the main altar. Its glow seemed to me to represent the spirit of Bernard Walke and I wondered what he would have thought if he had lived to see the great strides towards ecumenical acceptance in the year following the visit of the Pope to Britain.

Bernard Walke had, of course, braved the violence of the mob earlier in his career.

Through his membership of a peace society called 'The Fellowship of Reconciliation', he took part in campaigns, which included writing daily articles and letters to the press and attending meetings in London, Bristol and Liverpool as well as in many towns and villages in Cornwall.

One meeting held in the Labour Hall in Penzance, ended in uproar. While the meeting was in progress, 150 men of the Naval Reserve dressed in mufti, with an officer at their head, crowded into the hall.

'For an hour I struggled with this howling mob, while the officer stood by demanding that I would pledge my word never to speak again on the subject of peace.'

He refused to do this, so finally the officer jumped on a table and called on his men to sing *God Save the King*—which was apparently an arranged signal for breaking up the meeting.

As the women were hustled out, men laid hold of chairs, smashing them against the piano and throwing the pieces out of the windows.

Surrounded by this struggling mass of men, Bernard Walke attempted to leave the hall, but was overcome by a curtain, which was thrown over his head, and a blow which laid him out. When he came round, he found himself being defended by two soldiers—who told the crowd of fifty or more that they were willing to take on 'the whole bloody navy'. They wore 'wound stripes', and obviously made

The figure of Christ, carved by Phyllis Yglesias of Mousehole, is a memorial to Canon F. Rogers. The stone base was mutilated in the raid.

such an impression that the crowd allowed them to escort Walke and his party to a car.

The war held other hazards. For two years Walke was suspected by his neighbours of preparing for a landing on Marazion beach.

On one occasion a man who had driven him in his barouche-landau since the first day they had come to St Hilary, suddenly turned round on his box seat and shouted at him:

'You call yourself a parson, but you are nothing but a German spy. Half your pay do come from the Pope, and the other half from the Kaiser. You ought to hang from one of your tallest trees.'

These were the words of ignorance, fired by fear and suspicion—but as many, if not more, of the local populace, had reason to love him.

When the epidemic, which spread after the war, reached St Hilary, taking many victims, the parson and his wife visited, looked after the sick and housed them in an erstwhile pub called 'The Jolly Tinners'.

Memories of his own childhood probably influenced Walke—for the old Vicarage where he had been born, was previously 'The Black

Dog', and he remembers when they were children the door of the hall where they were playing being opened and a stranger calling for a pint of beer.

The Jolly Tinners became the Cornish Home for London Children—and housed children, who either had no parents, or were in various forms of trouble. The famous magistrate, Sir William Clarke Hall, who sat in Old Street Police Court and also conducted a Juvenile Court, often sent children to the Jolly Tinners, having committed them to Walke's care until they were sixteen, under an order of Court.

His children's home greatly benefited from the broadcasting of his plays on the BBC.

It began with the nativity play of *Bethlehem,* which was broadcast live from the church.

After the first production, a message came from Sir John Reith, director of the BBC, saying that Mr Ramsey MacDonald—the first Labour Prime Minister—had been dining with him, that they had listened to the play together, and wished to thank him for their

Father Walke with children at the Jolly Tinners.

beautiful presentation of the nativity.

Another venture in which Walke took a close interest was the attempt to re-open a mine, at a time when there was mass unemployment. Inspired from meetings with miners at the Friends Meeting Houses, the leading Christian bodies in Cornwall were contacted. Capital was promised, a deserted mine near Scorrier surveyed, and a service of dedication arranged.

A silver ring, chosen as 'a symbol of the marriage of men to industry under the blessing of the Church' was blessed, and then fifty miners took a vow before the Bishop and Ministers of different denominations, to share 'the Communion of the Ring in Cornwall'.

Despite promises of the capital needed to finance such a venture, the scheme finally fell because the Government's plans to relieve unemployment included road-making, and it was felt a rival scheme would be inopportune.

He had more success in helping tramps. He had his 'regulars'—the men, who are in Cornwall all the year round, who keep to their beat, usually between Truro and Land's End. A queer procession they would make, he says, if they could all be seen together—musicians who play on whistle pipes or accordians; men with trays of needles and thread; others without trays, who carry their stock in their hands; some without a leg, others without arms.

There was 'our Will', who was always quoting Shakespeare, and Jimmy who cut out pipe racks and photo frames with a fretsaw; Camborne Jack, with his insatiable needs and Old Williams, whose family came from Germoe, and who was originally said to have gone to Oxford, destined for the church. A Roman Catholic, he attended midnight Mass at Christmas dressed in a tall hat and frock coat, which he must have hired for the occasion. The laughter which greeted his appearance was not at his outfit—but the bottle of whisky sticking out of his coat tails!

One tramp took up residence on the vicarage lawn in a tent. This was Hope Johnson, who had asked Walke to buy him a pedlar's licence, as he wanted to walk round Cornwall, playing his flute and selling trinkets.

Unfortunately, the pedlar's licence, bought for him at a cost of 5s, could only be used after he had been three months in the county. Not being prepared to get a hawker's licence, costing £2, which would have enabled him to sell his goods at any time anywhere in

England, and not being able to take to the road without a licence, he continued to live in his tent on the lawn, practising on his flute and telling stories to the children at night.

He was finally driven away by the sheepdog, Driver, who insisted on sleeping in the tent with him.

'I would not mind if he had ordinary fleas,' he lamented, 'but they are elephants. They trample on me.'

Some of Bernard Walke's most enjoyable times were spent on the road, letting the donkey in his cart go where he pleased, and it must have been a strange sight to see the vicar pitched into the road, when the donkey would suddenly stop without warning, slide on his quarters with his hindlegs between his forelegs, and finally lie down and stretch on his side with his head on the ground as if dead. The only thing to do was to take the donkey out of the cart and re-harness him.

One donkey played this trick on him six times between St Hilary and Penzance. Gipsies and donkeymen suggested various ways of curing him, including lighting a fire to scare him—but an old Irish doctor supplied the answer. He told him to pour a few drops of water in the donkey's ear. This would set up such a tickle that he would have to get up to shake his head.

It worked like a dream, and ever afterwards he carried a phial of water in his waistcoat pocket, which he only had to bring out and show to the donkey, for him to be 'up and away'. Naturally local people thought it was holy water which drove the devil out of the donkey!

Not surprisingly, people did not take him for a parson when they met him in his old clothes, driving a painted shay. One day he was walking by the side of his donkey up Market Jew Street in Penzance on his way to Sennen, when he was joined by a queer looking fellow, carrying a black box on his shoulders, who suggested he should go into partnership with him.

When Walke asked him what he did, he replied he was 'in the mystery line'.

Said Walke: 'I'm in the mystery line too—I am the parish priest of a place called St Hilary.'

Replied the stranger: 'Whatever line you're in, you're a damned sight better liar than I am.'

Bernard Walke obviously thought his friend, Sandys Wason, was an eccentric. He said he pictured him as The White Knight in

Through The Looking Glass—or better still as the Confessor of Gnomes.

'There are few men living round whom so many legends have grown up as round Father Wason' he wrote.

Although some of the stories have little foundation, the fact that they are told and believed 'give him distinction in an age when so few achieve a personality to which it would be possible to attach any legend'. He says his whimsical nature is difficult to describe—'his scale of values is different and often disconcerting to his friends, as he is so impractical and aloof from ordinary affairs'.

Once when Walke was ill he received a telegram from Wason which read: 'Saying Mass for your intention tomorrow 10.30 am.'

The next morning he received another telegram: 'Too late, overslept. Tomorrow without fail.'

Another episode which involved a telegram concerned a dinner given by Compton Mackenzie and Faith to celebrate the publication of his book *Carnival.* Martin Secker, the publisher, proposed the toast, and while they were drinking Faith suggested that Father Wason should have been invited, as they had previously lived at Cury Vicarage. A telegram was sent, signed by all present, asking him to come. The reply received was: 'Have gone to bed to think over the best way to get to you.'

Walke describes a luncheon party Wason gave for him and some friends, including Dod and Ernest Proctor. They arrived, tired after a long bicycle ride, to find a notice pinned on the door saying 'No-one to enter'. After a time Wason came from the garden with his cassock tucked up round his waist and his arms full of irises. He made no attempt to welcome them, but hurried by, murmuring as he passed, 'Colour scheme for the table all wrong. Must get it right for Dod Proctor.'

After a further time of waiting and knocking on the door, an upstairs window was thrown up, and Father Wason shouted down: 'Table all wrong without a black centre. Am looking for my tall hat.'

After a further delay, the door was opened, they were greeted by Wason as if they had at that moment arrived, and were led to the dining room, where in the centre of the table was the tall hat filled with flowers.

'There was no hint of eccentricity in the tall hat as a table decoration, its shape and glossy blackness supplied a note that would otherwise have been lacking, so that one began to wonder why people had never thought of using tall hats as table centres before.

When he knew him in London he had bought an old-established church publishing firm, Cope and Fenwick. The name he said, was 'most distinguished and bound to bring customers'. The few customers, however, who did venture into the shop, were never encouraged to buy anything.

'What do you want?' he would say. 'Nothing here—all rubbish' and return to his breviary.

At other times he would adopt the manner of a businessman and sit at the telephone calling up booksellers all over London enquiring if they had some rare book or other in stock. He had no customers for these rare editions, but, he explained, it gave a good impression to the trade.

Father Wason ran into similar difficulties to Bernard Walke because of his extreme Catholic practices. He was eventually deprived of his living, which was declared vacant. The Bishop, however, was unwilling to go further, as an action for contempt of court would mean an indefinite term of imprisonment.

The local farmers had other ideas. 'We'll have 'en out,' they said. 'Like as we draw a badger.'

This they did—forcing an entry through the door, opened by Father Wason in expectation of a sick call.

His furniture was piled into wagons, and brought over to St Hilary. 'The parson over there is one of the same sort,' they said. 'Let him have his furniture.'

The goods were piled on so high, and so badly, that tables and chairs were swept off by the boughs of the trees as they came along the avenue.

Father Wason, who had arrived earlier with his housekeeper, who was clutching a roll of lavatory paper, refused to take any interest in his belongings, which were now being soaked by the rain, and continued his game of chess, saying it was 'clergymanly to fuss'.

All the furniture, which was covered in caterpillars, was piled in the house.

Father Wason left the next morning to return to Cury 'to say Mass for those stupid people'.

In a tribute to him Bernard Walke says: 'Looking back over the years since I first met Father Wason as an undergraduate, I regard him as not only the most original, but one of the most rare personalities that I have ever known.'

Parson Eccentrics

It's easy for a parson to be eccentric. If my theory holds good—that an eccentric is a person who does what he wants to do despite convention—then a clergyman has every opportunity to either be one, or become one.

In a way he is more or less a law unto himself.

He can order his day and his life entirely as he wishes; decide which services to hold, and the form they will take, whether to visit his parishioners, or never go near them, to be High Church, Low Church—or almost no church.

Lord Hugh Cecil told the Church Assembly that the Church of England is 'rich in eccentrics', and there is much evidence to back his assertion.

Writing about Parson Hawker of Morwenstow—a noted eccentric—Piers Brendon says that the Established Church in the nineteenth century attracted eccentrics 'or perhaps it would be truer to say that the Established Church, especially in rural areas, gave men, thus inclined, unique opportunities to cultivate their eccentricities'. He thinks this was particularly so in the diocese of Exeter—which then covered the whole of Cornwall—because in so large an area the bishop could not exert any real degree of control over his clergy.

Parson Hawker himself in his book *Footprints of Former Men* gives his own thoughts on why parsons of the seventeenth century were eccentric.

The church was in a transitory state, her ministers embodying a strange mixture of the old belief with the new interpretation; they were a long way from the civilising influence of London, the roads

◀Morwenstow Church

Parson Hawker: ' . . . eccentric in dress.'

were rough and rude, and their abodes in the wilds almost inaccessible.

'Hence it came to pass that the Cornish clergyman, insulated within his own limited sphere, often without even the presence of a country squire—and unchecked by the influence of the fourth estate, for until the beginning of the nineteenth century, 'Flindell's Weekly Miscellany' distributed from house to house from the pannier of a mule was the only reading matter—became developed about middle life into an original mind and man, sole and absolute within his parish boundary, eccentric when compared with his brethren in civilised regions.'

Whether Hawker actually acknowledged himself as an eccentric I do not know, but he certainly played up to visitors when his reputation became known. He told Sir Thomas Acland, a neighbour, that the bees on the cliffs picked up pebbles for ballast in high winds, dropping them at the entrance to their hives. He talked to the birds, giving them names like Jacky and Tommy; invited his nine cats into the church, and is said to have excommunicated one of them for killing a mouse on Sunday; had a pig as a constant companion and kept a couple of deer, called Robin Hood and Maid Marion. A visiting Low Church clergyman calling at the vicarage at Morwenstow was pinned to the ground by Robin's antlers, and had to be rescued by Hawker.

But there was no doubt of his eccentricities in dress. Over a blue, knitted fisherman's jersey, which had a small red cross woven into one side to mark the entrance of the centurion's spear, he wore a three-quarter-length claret or purple coloured coat. For extra warmth he would add a yellow poncho and scarlet gloves or gauntlets. He had a variety of hats, including a black velvet cap, a pink, brimless fez-like hat, and a 'wide-awake' of reddish brown.

He wore large, black or brown sea boots up to his knees, and his socks, made out of wool from his own ewe, were spun locally and knitted by girls at St Mark's School, Liskeard. He carried a walking stick shaped like a sword, with a cross at the top,a flat, carpenter's pencil, a bunch of seals with religious symbols to press on the wax of his letters, and wore medallions, one of which had been blessed by a Cardinal.

His indoor attire included a blue dressing gown, laced with gold braid, a vividly coloured biretta covered with sequins, and red slippers adorned with silver spangles.

When one of his fellow clergymen commented on his dress, he replied: 'At least I don't make myself look like a waiter or an unemployed undertaker.'

He had long hair—but hated beards; was proud of his ears which had no lobes—often remarking that the Duke of Wellington had ears of this shape, and that the feature could be traced in all the accurate pictures of Our Lord—and refused to wear false teeth when his own fell out, believing that all false teeth were taken by dentists from the jaws of human corpses, and that they 'decayed sympathetically' with the bodies of their original hosts.

His method of making tea was to fill the pot with tea leaves, and then pour the boiling water between the cracks. He liked the best ground coffee, but also loved cream—and was once discovered in the dairy at dead of night skimming off the thick cream from the previous day's milk with a spoon, and eating it as quickly as he could.

He had thick, woven paper with faint red lines on it specially made for him by De La Rue, and wrote on it with swan quills; and when he was writing in his hut on the cliffs, which he had made out of wood from wrecked ships, he would take a basket of ready filled pipes with him, saying that tobacco was 'the weed of thought'.

Parson Hawker wrote prolifically—his most famous ballad being *Trelawny*. Written under the title of *The Song of the Western Men*, it's well-known chorus asks:

And shall Trelawny die?
Here's twenty thousand Cornish men
Will know the reason why!

When the poem was published anonymously in 1825, it was thought by such judges as Dickens, Scott and Macaulay to be an original seventeenth-century popular song. But then he was said to have won the Newdigate Poetry Prize at Oxford by plagiarism, and to be an unreliable author, due to his habit of forging any documents he required for picturesque effect!

At the age of nineteen, Hawker wed a rich woman of 41, and after her death, married a young girl, forty years his junior, whose first impressions of him were that though 'a clever old soul' he was subject to the most absurd delusions and was 'slightly cracked'.

Equally famous in his eccentricity was the Rev. Frederick William Densham, who was at Warleggan Church from 1931 to 1953.

His unusual behaviour first seems to have manifested itself in the way he decorated the interior of the rectory, which he painted in red, yellow and blue. When he painted the church in the same colours at a cost of £50, the Bishop of Truro made him remove it at a further cost to Densham of £25.

Two years after his Induction, the parishioners' complaints, which were considered by the Bishop of Truro, included threatening to sell the organ, which had been given as a memorial to men in the

First World War; converting church property to his own use; refusing to hold services at convenient times; closing the Sunday School and putting a barbed wire fence round the rectory grounds. After hearing his explanations, the Bishop could see no reason to remove him, so the Church Council resigned as a body, and never went near the church again.

From this point on the rector's eccentricities became more pronounced. When no-one came to the church, he would lock it up and go down to the Methodist Chapel, where he told those present to abstain from drinking, playing cards, reading novels and going to the cinema.

After years of non-attendance at church by his parishioners—his entries in the Service Book would read 'No fog, no wind, no rain—no congregation'—he cut out figures in wood and cardboard and fixed them in the pews. These figures, whom he named after all the rectors of Warleggan, were preached to, offered the sacraments and given absolution.

He shut himself off in his rectory, allowed savage Alsatian dogs to roam in the grounds, dug a moat around a piece of land, where he said he wanted to be buried, and his servant was summoned to the house by a bell which rang in the stables.

When he died—lonely and alone—those looking at the house for the first time for over twenty years, found that every window had five different catches—one bedroom window could only be bolted from the *outside*—and every first-floor room had a pink cross painted on the door, with names like Siom, Alexandria and Pizgah. Under the drawing room a deep secret room was found.

Daphne du Maurier in her book *Vanishing Cornwall* tells the tale of the man who answered the Rector's advertisement for an organist. Arriving after dark, he found the rectory almost totally unfurnished, and the bedroom into which he was thrust, with the door locked on him, only contained packing cases against the walls and sacks on the floor. This might account for the room with the catch on the outside! The Rector is said to have taken him to church and conducted every service in the prayer book—afterwards feeding him on half a loaf of bread and corned beef.

After hearing this story, Dame Daphne visited Warleggan with a friend. They found the church desolated, but rang the bell at the rectory entrance gate. When eight or ten Alsatian dogs and wolfhounds sprang snarling upon the fence, they fled in terror.

On her next visit with two friends, the dogs had disappeared and they found the Rector walking in the garden. One of her friends waved a handkerchief at him. He paused, looked to left and right and stalked away, his hands behind his back.

The last time she visited Warleggan with her son, the Rector had died and the man who said he owned the house, after listening to her story of having seen Mr Densham walking up and down, told her softly: 'He still walks, back there in the garden . . .'

There is a happy ending to this sad tale, for the eccentric rector left quite a substantial sum to the Diocese. Called the Densham Car Loan Scheme, it provides between £4,000 and £5,000 a year to help clergy with the purchase of vehicles—as long as their own diocese match the amount proposed to be given with an equal sum.

One might almost say Densham rides again—in a very different form!

Ghosts are also associated with the next two eccentric

Warleggan Church: Densham preached to cardboard figures in the pews.

parsons—both of whom kept packs of hounds, and lived about the same time. The first was the Rev. Thomas Wills. He was the son of a Helston surgeon, Matthew Wills, who purchased the advowson of Wendron, which then also included Helston.

Because his father had wished it, Thomas took Holy Orders and was instituted in June, 1784. It is said that was the only time he occupied the pulpits of Wendron and Helston parish churches, and that he never again entered the churches all the 53 years he was vicar. This is obviously an exaggeration, for his signature has been found in the Marriage Register at least three or four times.

What is known is that he hunted, kept a pack of hounds at Trenethick, the old house just outside Helston where he lived, went badger baiting and attended local parish feasts.

He was also a great supporter of the week of sport held annually on Helston Downs, when such wrestling champions as Gundry, Rundle, Francis and Capel met all comers.

The Rev. Thomas Wills would join 'the quality' in their booths, where they feasted and 'wined' their friends, and subscribed prize money for the wrestling and racing. When he lay 'a-dying' it is said he enquired of a visiting friend how the 'wrastling' was going on the downs.

The Vicar, who was said to have had two illegitimate children, was written up in a poem by Captain Tobias Martin, a Wendron mine captain, who was quite a character. Called *Clerical Charity* it tells how the Vicar's cow died, and he was dissuaded from giving the flesh to his hounds as it might 'infect the kennels through'. Instead he sent a messenger round the parish announcing that there would be a free distribution of beef to the poor!

Opie's portrait of Wills, painted in Court suit with a sword, before he became Vicar of Wendron and Helston, was by the terms of his sister's will, taken out of the frame, rolled up and buried with her in the family vault at Helston.

The ghost of Wills is said to have haunted a windowless room at Trenethick house. Eventually a posse of parsons exorcised it at dead of night.

The second hunting and haunting parson was the Rev. Charles Lethbridge, appointed Rector of Stoke Climsland by the then Prince of Wales, later George IV, in 1805. He was devoted to the hunt and kept a pack of harriers.

Like his counterpart in Helston he was fond of good food and drink, and his language is said to have been at times 'more forcible than edifying'. Unlike the Rev. Thomas Wills, he was keen on church-going, and would drive his parishioners there, whether they wanted to or not—and not many would dare to give an excuse.

He had a great reputation as a ghost layer. One story tells of a woman who believed herself haunted by her mother's ghost, and used to send to the Rector at all hours of day and night to exorcise it. The ghost, however, was invariably gone when he arrived.

At last the Rector questioned the woman. Had she always been a good daughter, he asked?

She said she had—though added it was true that when her mother had been 'that aggravating' she had taken her by the hair and dragged her down the stairs, bumpety bump, until she reached the bottom. Hearing this, the Rector declared the ghost had great reason on its side, and he wouldn't try to get rid of it any more. The woman then became penitent, and soon after the ghost ceased its haunting.

A vicar of more recent years in a parish on the banks of the Fal might have given his own church the reputation of having a ghost. For he slept by day and did his parish visiting by night, finishing up by playing the church organ from midnight onwards, with his unmarried sister, with whom he lived, asleep in the pews.

In the far reaches of Cornwall in the parish of Sennen, another clergyman became an eccentric by neglect. He was the Rev. William Spry, who was the curate at the church from 1816 to 1826.

He served St Levan as well, but lived in Penzance, and so was at quite a distance from the parishes in which he was supposed to minister. The mode of transport he adopted was a wooden horse, which was propelled by the feet along the ground. He could be seen thrusting his velocipede along, with his dog, Sport, who went everywhere with him, running alongside.

If the weather was bad, he stayed at home in Penzance, so often there was no-one to conduct the services at either church. Neglect took its toll, and there were said to be weeds growing in the pews, and his surplice to be a mixture of rags and iron-mould.

Today the church looks spick and span. If you go, have a look at the stained-glass window commemorating John Gifford Everett JP. He was thirteen times Mayor of Wells in Somerset; was a visitor to the parish for fifty years, building Hallan House at Land's End, and died in 1917 in his hundredth year.

Nowadays Bishops do not tend to be as eccentric as the

clergymen under them—well, not the ones I've met, anyway—but Bishop Hunkin was certainly 'a character' verging on the eccentric—while his father was definitely one.

Joseph Weston Hunkin was a coal merchant. The family were quite well off at one time, being the owners of three ships, and living at The Parade in Truro—that delightful row of Regency houses, above Malpas Road.

The Hunkin family fortunes declined, however, and from being a proud ship-owner, Mr Hunkin drove a coal wagon, calling out: 'Hunkin's coal. I'm the man who dropped the price and kept it down.'

He was best known as a preacher 'fervent, extrovert and un-self-conscious'. He would begin services on street corners by simply spreading his handkerchief on the ground and falling on his knees. He led the singing at the Gwennap Pit rallies, and would begin to sing a hymn anywhere. This is probably why his son, as Archdeacon of Coventry, was able, when a bedridden lady in a workhouse mentioned she liked a certain hymn, to sing it to her unaccompanied.

If he had a preaching assignment, he would arrive at the place an hour before the time of the service, and walk up and down the street, singing hymns and inviting everyone he saw to come to the chapel. The story is related that in Chacewater, customers sitting in a barber's shop on a Sunday suddenly found themselves being kissed by Mr Hunkin, and then invited to come to his service.

At business he wore a suit of black broadcloth, a cravat instead of a tie and a chain supporting a great silver turnip watch. If someone swore at work, he would say to them: 'Excuse me, you have spoken lightly of my best friend.'

When he moved to London to live with his daughter, he would talk with every stranger he met. His questions to them included; 'Have you been saved?', 'Have you seen the light?'. On one of his walks in the park, he was seen to challenge 22 people in this way.

A London policeman, busily engaged in directing traffic on Hanwell Broadway, became very interested professionally when he said he had 'found a pearl of great price'! A young girl who was offered his knee in a crowded London bus, surprised him by suspecting his motives.

In his early seventies he went to the cinema for the first time—but said he would never go again, in case he was called to his Maker while he was in such an ungodly place.

His son, despite his Methodist upbringing, became Bishop of Truro. Throughout his life he made notes on odd scraps of paper, and his sermons were often written on the backs of cathedral service lists.

He learnt to drive when he was serving in Rugby as Archdeacon of Coventry, and his driving became notorious—some might even say reckless. He usually pressed the starter on the dashboard with his foot, and had a theory that if you rushed across crossroads, your chances of a collision were more remote.

When he went to London he stayed at the YMCA, and his son can remember seeing him absent-mindedly raising his umbrella as the train rushed into a tube station. There was the time, too, when he sat waiting on the steps of Westminster Abbey with his hat beside him—only to find that people were kindly throwing in pennies!

His maiden speech in the House of Lords was about the Home Guard. He served in it as a private, and when on guard or fire-watching he would read the Greek Testament.

When he was working in Rugby he told a curate that he hadn't been able to prepare a sermon, so proposed instead to read extracts from *Pilgrim's Progress*.

He once crossed a cheque by mistake, and instead of writing 'pay cash', wrote 'uncrossed' on the line.

He will always be remembered for his visit to the Bishop Rock lighthouse, where he was to confirm two keepers. He was hauled up in the same way as they were, with the rope fastened round his body and wearing his black frock coat and gaiters.

A sporting parson was the Rev. Jack Parsons—a clerical cricketer. He played for Warwickshire, remembers bowling to W.G. Grace, and at a dinner in London given by the Cricket Society, jumped on a table—although he was then over eighty—and demonstrated the back lift and follow-through necessary to drive a fast ball over the bowler's head to the boundary.

He spent his seventieth birthday batting in the Edgbaston nets, and three weeks later played for the Warwickshire Old County Cricketers Association against Solihull School. He scored 65 in 43 minutes before being stumped. His score included four sixes, and his drives 'stung the hands of those who tried to catch him!' He then took an evening train to watch the Lord's Test.

He played with, or against, the 'greats' in cricket.

Larwood said of him that he was 'a beautiful cricketer and a punishing batsman'. While playing for the MCC against Wrekin School in 1935 the two young members of the groundstaff included in the team were D.C.S. Compton and W.J. Edrich. He played against Hutton in his last county match a year earlier.

As a chaplain in the army in the Second World War he drove around in an Army baby Austin, out of which his head stuck through the open roof, well above windscreen height. He defied the Geneva Convention by carrying a revolver, and was upset because he was never posted to the front line—even though he was 49 when the war began.

In North Africa he established the custom of a chaplains' conference every Monday morning in Algiers, after which there would be lunch and a bathe in the Mediterranean. This became known as 'The Bishops' Bathe', though no Bishop was ever involved.

Jack Parsons returned to Liskeard in the autumn of 1944, having only served a few months as their parish priest in 1939. His bluff man-to-man approach went down well with the farmers, and he would go to Liskeard market and consult them about the best time to have the Harvest Thanksgiving Service.

To one young reporter from the *Cornish Times* getting her Monday morning copy and showing her cynicism for church matters he said: 'I'm sick of you people who stand on the touch line and judge—why don't you come into the game and do something about it?'

She did—and became one of the parish's most faithful members.

An action of his in 1958, a little while before he left the town shows his courage and attracted considerable press coverage. A teddy boy, who had been drinking, came into St Martin's club, which the Vicar ran. He started swearing in front of the girls, threatened to 'knock the vicar's block off' and refused to leave. Parsons simply picked him up and threw him out. Next day the young man turned up at the Vicarage, apologised and asked if he could join the club. His application was gladly accepted, and his first year's sub was paid by the Vicar.

Always regarded as a 'larger than life figure', he brought his personality to bear on even the smallest actions. A friend remembers watching him buy an umbrella: 'It is difficult to imagine a more mundane operation when performed by an ordinary person—but when Parsons did it, it became fascinating. He took

The Rev. Parsons, ploughs a Cornish field with a ploughshare forged from an enemy sword. 'And their swords shall be turned into ploughshares!'

each one in turn and tested it—playing a variety of superbly executed cricket strokes—going forward to a ball that had been well pitched up, turning a ball to fine leg, making a late cut which nearly demolished a glass case. Eventually, after a further testing for balance, he made his choice. Only after he had walked out of the shop, carrying his new umbrella on his shoulder did I realise that the only thing he had not done had been to open it to see how it functioned as an umbrella.'

Another parson connected with balance is Canon Dr Howard Miles Brown, Vicar of St Winnow and St Veep. He is a clock expert, and not only does he repair antique clocks—but he also constructs them. The cuckoo clock he made once was so realistic, that neighbours hearing the sound reported they had never heard the bird at such an early date!

He repaired the count house clock from the Levant Mine, which is now housed in the County Museum, Truro, and made a combined astronomical calendar, planetarium and musical clock over a period of ten years.

He has a Bachelor of Science degree in engineering, and started his career as a civil engineer with Plymouth Corporation. He lived in Saltash at the time, and taught himself Greek and Hebrew as he travelled between stations.

My last personality could be said to have become an eccentric after his death. He was Francis Tregian of Golden, near Probus—the first Englishman to shelter a Catholic priest from the law and to pay the full penalty.

One of his main 'crimes' was to refuse an offer of a viscountcy from Queen Elizabeth I. He gave as his reasons that 'the burden of nobility' would be too great, and that he was really interested in furthering the cause of the true Catholic religion.

Some days later, late at night, a maid of honour came to his chamber bearing a message from the Queen. He was to go to her at once—there were urgent matters she wished to discuss with him. He said he was unwell, and begged to be excused. Not long afterwards she was by his side, showing great concern for his health.

Once again she asked him to accept a viscountcy. Again he refused, and made the mistake of offering her his fortune instead. The Queen was enraged, so he made his escape in the middle of the night, believing discretion in this case to be the better part of valour. Like any woman scorned, the Queen then got her own back.

She declared him a traitor, and the story is a sorry one after that of great hardship through imprisonment, of confiscation of his property and banishment. He finally finished up in Lisbon, where he obtained sanctuary with the Jesuit fathers at San Roque.

After his death in 1608 he was buried in the church of San Roque. The inscription on his tomb reads: 'In this vault is interred Mr Francis Tregian, an English gentleman who was detained 28 years for the holy faith in England. He was lord of many vassals, but they took from him all his estate. At last, being exiled from England, he came to his city of Lisbon where he lived on an allowance of 60 crowns a month given him by the king. At 60 years of age our Lord took him to Paradise on the 28th September, 1608.'

In 1625 the stones covering the tomb were removed. The body of a young man who had been buried there five years earlier was found to have disintegrated, but Francis Tregian's body was as fresh as the newly dead body waiting to be buried above it.

An English resident in Lisbon at the time wrote to a friend in Madrid on the day following the opening of the tomb. The grave of the English knight, he said 'being opened yesterday, his body was found incorrupt and entire, without corruption in any part, so much as in nose, ears or stomach . . . yea, even his bowels were whole, neither did any evil savour or smell proceed from it.

'His hair is upon his head and beard, his flesh soft, and being pressed down riseth up again; his arms, fingers and legs flexible.

'Finally, all who have resorted here—physicians and others—judge the matter to be miraculous, for it is 17 years since he was buried . . . some have confessed they endeavoured to pull off the fingers and nails, but could not.

'Also, another particular circumstance happened to be found, and was that all the Franciscan habit wherein he was buried was consumed, save only so much as was sufficient to cover his members—about a span in length and breadth, which was found entire.'

When news of the discovery spread, there was much excitement in the city—especially when the miraculous powers of the body became known. Some pulled out hairs from the head and beard; some cut off tiny parts of the remaining piece of garment; others scraped up a handful of earth from round the tomb.

It was reported that one man became freed of a daily fever and severe headaches by pressing a handful of the earth against his skin.

A nobleman plucked six hairs from Tregian's head—two of his daughters used the hairs and were cured of their maladies, one being on the point of death. A footman to Don Gondisali Vaz Coutinho had his legs cured of virulent ulcers; a beggar in the same house was freed of a fever which had plagued him on and off for two years. A nun of the Convent of St Clare placed a hair from the body's beard on her stomach, and was relieved of sickness and quinsy. And so the reports went on.

It was decided that the Tregian family should be informed of the discovery, but relations were not easy to find. A daughter, Philippa, was finally traced to Ireland, where she was living with her husband, Father James Plunket, and she was sent a piece of the cloth.

The miracles began again. First of all Philippa's mother-in-law had a fever cured. Then when a man died without the last sacrament, Father Plunket, who was the man's confessor, prayed with the help of the cloth that the dead man might come back to life, receive the sacrament, be absolved of his sins and then die again—happily. The man, Griffin Evans, did come back to life 'with a deep sigh', and the rites being performed 'paid the debt of nature once again'.

Father Plunket going from Ireland to England with his father and brother in a ship, which was one of a company of seven making the crossing, got caught in a great storm. The other six ships went down, and the captain of their ship leapt into a small boat to try and save himself. Father Plunket then threw his miracle cloth on the waves. Immediately, the waters were calmed, the wind dropped, the waves ceased their roaring and the ship was able to reach its destination.

Today at Golden can be seen the remains of those Tudor mansions in which the Tregians lived—a reminder of a man who was prepared to suffer greatly for his faith, but whose additional claim to fame was the miraculous preservation of his body, an eccentricity of a rather unusual kind.

Acknowledgements

Without libraries to consult, I don't know how most authors would manage—so my very grateful thanks to Terry Knight and Barbara Olds of the Local Studies Library, Redruth and to Leslie Douch and the staff of the Royal Institution of Cornwall in Truro.

I owe a great debt to the Bishop of Truro, the Rt. Rev. Peter Mumford, for coping so good-naturedly with my 'eccentric' queries in the middle of a very busy life. Also for the help received from the Rev. Desmond Curson, Rector of St Hilary, and Arthur Olavesen, who was a mine of information on the subject of that church.

My thanks to Michael Williams for his advice and encouragement and to Colin Wilson, for his contribution in the midst of getting his own books to press. I would also like to thank Michael Joseph Ltd for their kind permission to use material from *Canon's Folly* by Canon Martin Andrews.

I can't thank the living subjects of this book enough for agreeing to be put under my microscope and labelled 'eccentric'. René Halkett, whose drawings were recently published for the first time, became a valued friend in the short time I knew him, and the editing of the piece on himself was probably one of the last things he wrote.

Lastly, I would like to dedicate this book to my mother and my mother-in-law. Both were born in the same year, and both spent their last years in Cornwall. But as people they were totally different. My mother—gentle, shy and retiring, with her own brand of humour. My mother-in-law—a real character, perceptive, witty and lively. I would like to think this book is a small remembrance to them, as they lie near each other in Mylor Churchyard.

Books Consulted

Andrews, Martin. *Canon's Folly.* Michael Joseph.
Boyan, P.A. and Lamb, G.R. *Francis Tregrian.* Sheed & Ward.
Brendon, Piers. *Hawker of Morwenstowe.* Jonathan Cape.
du Maurier, Daphne. *Vanishing Cornwall.* Gollancz.
Dunstan, Alan and Peart-Binns, John S. *Cornish Bishop.* Epworth Press.
Hawker, R.S. *Footprints of Former Men in Cornwall.* John Lane.
Howat, Gerald. *Cricketer Militant.* North Moreton Press.
Peter, Thurstan C. *Collins's History of Cornwall.* Netherton & Worth.
Rendell, Joan. *Cornish Churches.* Bossiney Books.
Rowse, A.L. *A Cornishman Abroad.* Jonathan Cape.
Walke, Bernard. *Twenty Years at St Hilary.* Methuen.

ALSO AVAILABLE

VIEWS OF OLD CORNWALL
by Sarah Foot

A CORNISH CAMERA
by George Ellis and Sarah Foot

THE CORNISH YEAR BOOK

CURIOSITIES OF CORNWALL
by Michael Williams

CORNWALL IN UPROAR
by David Mudd

GHOSTS OF CORNWALL
by Peter Underwood

THE CALL OF THE WEST
by Arthur Caddick

CASTLES OF CORNWALL
by Mary and Hal Price

LEGENDS OF CORNWALL
by Sally Jones

AROUND LAND'S END
by Michael Williams

CORNISH CHURCHES
by Joan Rendell

THE CORNISH EDWARDIANS
by David Mudd

THE CRUEL CORNISH SEA
by David Mudd

DISCOVERING CORNWALL'S SOUTH COAST
by E.V. Thompson

KING ARTHUR COUNTRY
by Brenda Duxbury, Michael Williams
and Colin Wilson

STRANGE HAPPENINGS IN CORNWALL
by Michael Williams